A Class of Their Own

Tom Ervin

The Inside Story of the Great Lakes 70 Fleet

©2008 Tom Ervin
Publication Design & Cover by Mark Hammermeister
ISBN 978-0-9778759-1-7
First Printing: March 2008

FORWARD

—◖◖◗—

By Sam Nedeau
Executive Director of the Great Lakes 70s Sailing Association

In the fall of 2006, Al Fletcher, the owner of the Great Lakes 70 COLT 45, contacted me about a Detroit area sailor who was interested in doing a book on the GL 70s. It is not uncommon for sailors to contact our class with the expectation of catching a ride or utilizing the class to promote a product or themselves. Al explained that this sailor, Tom Ervin, had written a book about his experience in the 2005 Bayview Mackinac race and was interested in doing the same for our class.

I contacted Tom to discuss his idea and he immediately distinguished himself from the others. He explained to me that his sailing resume did not qualify him for a crew spot aboard our boats. He further told me he was not young, but that he was willing to get in the requisite physical condition necessary to assure that he would not be a liability. It was apparent that he and his idea were worth exploring. I invited him to attend the fall owners meeting to present his idea. The owners immediately approved his proposal, and with that, Tom had set himself up for a season of GL 70 racing; something that plenty have attempted but few have succeeded in doing.

Tom is a better sailor than he represented. While he could have been a vocal crewmember, he did a masterful job of blending in and fulfilling the role of Indian rather than Chief. He stood his watch and never needed to be beckoned twice when his talents were called upon. He was a crewmember, not an imbedded journalist. After the races he coiled lines and asked questions about how to improve and what else he could do. On shore he did not overstate his onboard role to the competitors and he never 'got over served.' He remained grateful for his opportunity and dedicated to his promise. In many ways his enthusiasm was contagious, though that was not his goal.

At the conclusion of the season, I spoke to several of the Great Lakes 70s sailors with whom Tom had sailed. Each discussed Tom's presence as that of a crewmember and not an invited guest.

Congratulations, Tom! Book or no book, you are a Great Lakes 70 sailor and we hope to sail with you again someday.

ACKNOWLEDGEMENTS

I want to thank everyone involved with the Great Lakes 70 Sailing Association for their many kindnesses extended to me and for their help in assembling the many details included herein.

Many thanks also go to Jack Jennings for his willingness to invite me aboard PIED PIPER for the 2007 Chicago to Mackinac Race as well as his role as Contributing Editor to this book.

Most importantly, my heartfelt thanks to my wife Nancy for her support and enthusiasm for my pursuit of yet another adventure.

TABLE OF CONTENTS

THE LONGEVITY OF THE GREAT LAKES 70 SAILING ASSOCIATION

By Sam Nedeau
Executive Director of the Great Lakes 70s Sailing Association

There are several reasons for the success of the class. There are undeniable elements such as the boats themselves and the waters we sail upon that lend to the success. Remember, however, these very same boats campaigned on the West Coast and their class fell apart and consequently moved to the Great Lakes. Over the years, I believe that there have been 10 to 15 primary reasons that the class has enjoyed such success and longevity. Those 10 to 15 reasons are the owners themselves. Each brings a significant amount of sailing experience and knowledge to the table. Each has been around the block, campaigned boats of various sizes and could be described as a sailing lifer. When it comes to sailing, these owners have been there and done that. Each is also very success-ful professionally which results in the owner's meetings somewhat reflecting a Fortune 500 board meeting.

The one thing each owner has in common is the insistence that the class be well represented with capable leadership. Fortu-nately, Dick Jennings and Peter Reichelsdorfer have been leading the class for several years. Dick assessed the demise of the West Coast sleds (The GL70 boats are nicknamed SLEDS because they are long and narrow and built to run downhill, before the wind.) He concluded it was due to the fact that the boats ended up in an arms race in an effort to go faster. Dick and Peter have remained steadfast in preventing the turboing of our boats. The boats are plenty fast already and the ability to sail head-to-head is of paramount importance in keeping the class together.

The class has also enjoyed great camaraderie over the years. This is not by coincidence. Years ago, when Dick Jennings appointed me to my position, he discussed the importance of the social element and of maintaining the camaraderie. We have after-race gatherings, as do other classes. What makes the difference for the GL70s is that the owners and crews all respect each other. In short, I believe that the owners and crews all believe that they have inside information, and that information is that this class and these boats are special. These owners have built and owned Farr 40s, IOR boats, PHRF boats, IMS boats, one designs and one offs and here they are in the GL70 class. The crews have sailed in multiple programs and on many different boats. They all will tell you that sailing Macs or going into a mark overlapped on the 70s is a thrill unequalled by any other sailing. I recall an American Express commercial where the catch line is 'Membership has its privileges.' The same can be said for this class. The owners and crews are experienced enough to know it.

THE DEAL

"Some men see things as they are and ask why. Others dream things that never were and ask why not."

—*George Bernard Shaw*

I've always been a dreamer. To my good fortune, my dreams have almost always been realized. Most people either don't have dreams at all or have dreams but won't permit themselves to pursue them. I think that's most unfortunate. Remember, this life is not a rehearsal. If there is something you want to do or become, why not go for it?

I married the girl of my dreams and she has graciously allowed me to pursue my dreams throughout our 43 year marriage. As a result, I started seven businesses from scratch and—other than two brief interludes working for someone else—have always been an entrepreneur.

I turned 58 in 1999 and, after a thirty-year absence, I re-entered the sport of sailing by racing 19' Lightnings on Cass Lake outside the city of Detroit. As a member of the Pontiac Yacht Club, I really got into small boat racing against similar boats every Wednesday night and Sunday morning during the season. Over a six year period, I and my partner, Wylie Gerdes, were out there competing in a total of approximately 150 races. We had the greatest time. Because it was the largest Lightning Club in the world, we regularly had 20 boats or more on the starting line. Many of the members

Racing my Lightning on Cass Lake.

were state, regional and some national champions in the Lightning Class. So, the competition was strong and spirited. During these years, I was managing a high-risk software business I had founded in January of 1998. The financial risks were enormous. When I stepped onto that yellow sailboat, however, all my business worries were forgotten and I had only one thing on my mind. GO FAST! No one should be allowed to have the great fun I had on Cass Lake.

In June of 2005, my mind turned to the upcoming Bayview Yacht Club's annual Port Huron to Mackinac Race, which covers all of Lake Huron from Port Huron, Michigan to Mackinac Island, located at the very tip of the State of Michigan in the Mackinac Straits, a distance of 254 nautical miles.

I had always envied those 3,000 sailors who made the trek up the lake each July. I was now 63 years old and had very little experience in the big boats (27' and up) which raced to Mackinac. I also thought, however, that I could never really call myself a sailor if I hadn't done at least one Mackinac Race.

I called an owner of a 35' boat with whom I had done a little sailing three years prior and asked if he needed another crewman for the race. The owner, Doug Livermore, was very kind and allowed me onboard despite my limited experience. Well, it turned out to be the most exciting adventure in my sailing career as a large storm hit the fleet with 27 knot winds and eight foot waves for eight hours.

It was such an incredible experience for me that I was compelled to write a book about it entitled *VICTORY*. To my great surprise, I learned that it was the first book ever written about this particular race in its 82 year history. Although I had written other books dealing with the real estate industry, this was my first book about yacht racing. I have always enjoyed writing and was a nationally syndicated real estate columnist for 20 years. I guess I picked up the joy of writing from my mother who raised six kids while writing many short stories and two books, one fiction, one non-fiction.

The story I'm about to tell you is true. It is the result of my most recent dream—to race on a Great Lakes 70 racing yacht in a Chicago to Mackinac Race. Although I can best be described as an average sailor, I knew I didn't have the racing credentials which would justify a crew position on one of these boats. Despite my lack of sailing skills, I still wondered what it would be like sailing at the top of the sport on the largest boats, with the best crews against the greatest competition on the Great Lakes.

These boats are 68' long, have a 15' beam and are owned by great racing yachtsmen. There are ten of them located on the Great Lakes and represent, to my knowledge, the only one design fleet of racing yachts this large anywhere in the world.

I had already sailed in the 2005 Bayview Port Huron Mackinac Race and would have loved to complete the circuit by racing on one of these boats in the other Mackinac race, The Chicago to Mackinac Race. It is the longest annual fresh water yacht race in the world, beginning just off Navy Pier in downtown Chicago and terminating on the same Mackinac Island, 289.4 nautical miles up the length of Lake Michigan.

At the age of 65, I certainly wasn't getting any younger. I had just completed a satisfactory annual physical and felt that if I was going to make this dream come true, time was of the essence. I then began to ask myself, "Is there a way to make it happen?" I knew that the ten owners of these boats had formed an association, called the GL70 Sailing Association, headquartered in Chicago. After mulling it over for a couple of weeks in August of 2006, I came up with an idea which I thought just might work.

I called Allan Fletcher, the owner of COLT 45, one of the ten boats in the GL70 Class, which he kept during the season near his home in Alpena, Michigan. I met Allan while writing about his victory in my book about the 2005 Bayview Mackinac Race. That year he won in the GL70 Class and was also the overall winner of that year's race. I asked him if he could get me on the agenda for the fall meeting of the Association, which would be conducting its meeting the following month. He contacted the Association's Executive Director, Sam Nedeau. I was invited to attend the meeting and was given a spot near the end of the agenda. The meeting was held at Shaw's Crab House in Downtown Chicago on September 21, 2006.

THE DEAL

When my turn on the agenda arrived, I passed out a copy of *VICTORY* to each person. Three of the owners had already read the book, for which I was very grateful. They were also complimentary about it, which gave me some credibility with the others. I began by admitting to all of them that I did not possess sailing skills in any way comparable to theirs. I did, however, despite that fact, have a proposal to offer them.

PIED PIPER RACING
PIED-PIPER.COM

This is my photo as a crewman aboard PIED PIPER, taken on the morning of July 14, 2007, a few hours before the beginning of Chicago Yacht Club's "Race to Mackinac." The boat was docked at Burnham Harbor in downtown Chicago with Soldier Field in the background.

My proposition was a simple one: "If one of the owners would allow me to participate on their boat as a crewman for the 2007 Mackinac Race, I would write a book about my experience and the GL70 Class so that they would have a keepsake to hand down to their children and grandchildren."

There was a brief silence in the room, which was quickly interrupted by the voice of a young man seated to my left. It was the voice of Jack Jennings, skipper of the GL70 PIED PIPER. He simply said, "Tom, you'll come with us on PIED PIPER!"

In that brief moment, my dream was realized.

Little did I know the magnitude of the great adventure I had undertaken. I was about to see and be a part of a sailing program few sailors would ever experience in their careers. I would also meet inspiring people who would give me the opportunity to relearn, once again, all the important lessons of life.

THE 2007 GL70
CHICAGO TO
MACKINAC RACE

PIED PIPER approaching Navy Pier before the start.

July 14, 2007, 12:00PM CDT
CHICAGO TO MACKINAC RACE COURSE

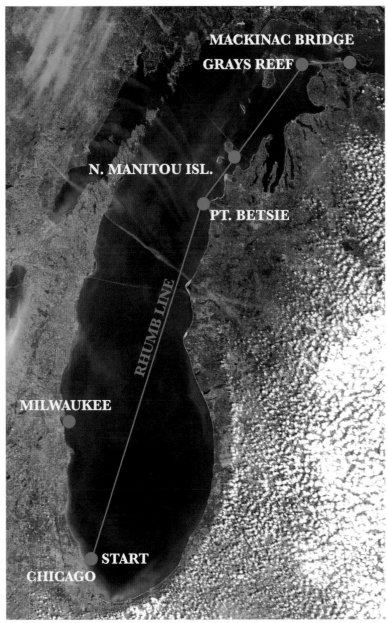

Photo courtesy of Liam Gumley, Space Science and Engineering Center, University of Wisconsin-Madison.

What an incredible sight! I'm standing behind Jack Jennings (Jack's biography, page 127) at the helm of PIED PIPER. Because of the strong 30 knot winds, the boat is powered up and, with a good angle of heel, heading for the waters just east of Navy Pier in downtown Chicago. At last, the one day, which only comes once a year, has arrived. It's the beginning of the annual sprint up the length of Lake Michigan by hundreds of racing yachts and thousands of sailors; the sailing of Chicago Yacht Club's "Race to Mackinac."

We're a couple hours away from the start of the longest annual freshwater race in the world. I'm a member of the thirteen-man crew of PIED PIPER, one of only ten boats which compete in their own class, the Great Lakes 70 Sailing Association. With the exception of two other racing yachts, these boats (known as GL70's) are the largest on the Great Lakes. They are known for their great skippers, crews and tremendous speed capabilities.

I'm a 65 year old on a boat with a crew comprised primarily of twenty somethings led by a 27 year old skipper. As we make our approach to sail past the end of the pier, a large cruise ship pulls away from the dock and is headed toward a spot where both boats might converge. The other skipper gives us the right of way and we continue without changing course to our destination. Part of the tradition of the Chicago Race is the parade by Navy Pier of the boats proceeding to the starting area about one mile off shore.

Before we left the dock, our crew had temporarily rigged a boom box on the floor of the cockpit with loud speakers. Moments later, while motoring out of Burnham Harbor, the boom box is blaring that great theme from the *Rocky* movies, "Gonna Fly Now." The music puts everyone in great spirits. Now, as we approach the end of Navy Pier, we're playing, "Living in America." Hundreds of people are crowding the rail of Navy Pier to get a good look at the boats and crews heading to the starting line. They are yelling and waving at us and we're yelling and waving back at them. It was one

Jack Jennings & crew aboard PIED PIPER.

of those moments that can only be described as a great celebration
of life itself. After all the months of work, great expense and
meticulous planning, we are on our way to commit our boat, our
skills and our passion to a fierce competition with like-minded
sailors on nine other boats, each with a storied history of winning.

   Although all ten boats are quite similar, our skipper and crew
is very different than the others. Jack Jennings, our skipper, the
son of the founder of the Great Lakes 70 Association and an
internationally known yachtsman, finds himself competing
with his father's peers, each with thirty to sixty years of racing
experience. After years of sailing with his dad, Jack became
the skipper of **PIED PIPER** in 2005. During his 2006 sailing
season, **PIED PIPER** won the Chicago NOOD Regatta and
finished second in the Bayview Mackinac Race. During his first
couple of racing seasons as skipper, Jack worked at building
his own crew. Some were existing members who had sailed

In the PIED PIPER crew photo above, beginning on the left is Dave Shriner, Eric Jochum, Tom Ervin, Brian Brophy, Bob Wiesen, (above Bob) Dave Jochum, skipper, Jack Jennings, Eric ViGrass, (above Eric) Ben Biddick, Andy McCormick, (above Andy) Mike Hoey, Perry Lewis and J.B. Schumaker.

aboard the boat for many years. Others were new to the boat. The biggest qualities Jack was looking for were a strong team orientation and experience on winning boats. On most racing boats, and especially on large boats such as the GL70 which carries a crew of 12 to 15 people, effective team work is essential for the best results. Some of the features of the GL70, which appeal to Jack, are tremendous boat speed optimized for sailing on the Great Lakes and good balance on all points of sail.

In 2006, Jack established **PIED PIPER** Racing, LLC and built a web site to follow all of the events and experiences of the **PIED PIPER** Team. He also hopes it will bring sailing to a wider audience by working with organizations inside and outside the sailing community. He plans to use sailing as a marketing or branding vehicle. Jack continues to help run Smithereen Pest Management Company, his family's pest control business of which he is the fourth generation owner since its founding in 1888.

The weather forecast is for 30 knot winds out of the southwest. If the forecast holds true, it will be a fast start to a very long race. Everyone on the water is looking forward to it. The wind is so strong that, once we get into the starting area we can see some boats have already reefed in their mainsails, which help keep the boat from heeling over too far. We take our sails down, turn on the engine and have lunch.

Jack Jennings

On these big boats, each crewman has a primary responsibility in which he has demonstrated proficiency. Another member of the **PIED PIPER** team, Bob Wiesen (Bio, page 147) is the pit man, which means he controls the two winches used to raise and lower the spinnaker pole. He stands on the main companionway steps leading down to the cabin below. The winches are located either side of the companionway. He is also involved when sails are changed and brought below for repacking.

He is also the provisioner and cook on **PIED PIPER**. Bob makes huge sandwiches that definitely take two hands. He plans his meals based upon the protein and carbohydrates the crew needs to keep up its strength and energy. His job is vital to success on a long distance race. **PIED PIPER** doesn't permit individual beverage bottles to be brought aboard in distance races, so, everyone drinks out of common water and Kool Aid jugs, which are passed from one crewman to the next. The boat has no refrigeration system and only a two burner stove to comply with the rules. Removing the refrigeration system saved 75 pounds and the original, larger stove was eliminated with an additional 35 lbs. savings. With these limitations it is necessary to carefully plan meals which don't require refrigeration.

Heavy wind and waves prior to the start with Chicago skyline in the background.

Although there are 290 boats in this race, only 20 or so are sent off the starting line at a time, each group following the previous one in ten minute intervals. The first group goes off at 12:00 p.m. CDT. Typically, the smallest boats are first and each group thereafter is larger in length. Our group has a starting time of 2:20 p.m., followed by the last group comprised of catamarans and trimarans. At approximately 1:40 p.m., lunch is over and Jack decides to raise our mainsail

in preparation for the start. At this time, the wind is howling
and the starting area is still crowded with other boats
constantly moving back and forth awaiting their start times.

The huge U.S. Coast Guard Cutter MACKINAW is standing by.
It is a tradition for the Coast Guard to assign one of its larger ships
to each Mackinac Race. It remains stationary near the starting line
until all racers are underway and proceeding northward. Its job is
to trail the fleet throughout the race in order to be available to help
boats in distress. The MACKINAW never dropped its anchor, nor
did it change its position despite the heavy seas. It is equipped with
a new Global Positioning System (GPS), which automatically relays
to the power and steering controls of the boat the exact global
position the boat is to maintain. With its bow pointed into the
wind, the steering and propeller provide just the amount of power
needed for the boat to maintain its position.

Jack decides to motor around behind the cutter (to leeward)
where the high profile of the boat will protect us from the wind
while we raise our mainsail. It works well. We can see a canopy
installed on the stern of the MACKINAW, packed with various
dignitaries who have a great view of the proceedings. With our
mainsail fully raised, we sail out from behind the cutter and
begin assessing the length and precise location of the starting line.
There are a number of floating buoys and many sailboats and
small motorized spectator boats in the starting area, which can
make identifying the starting line confusing. Perry Lewis, a sail
maker with North Sails in Chicago and extensive Mackinac racing
experience, is also a member of the crew. He helps Jack assess the
starting line and discusses our starting strategy. With about twenty-
five minutes remaining before our start, the engine is turned off
and we sail under the mainsail only.

For the start, Jack asks me to stand behind him at the helm. This
is to allow the more experienced members of the crew to handle
the vital functions needed to execute as successful a start as possible.

Ben Biddick working the grinder.

Suddenly, behind me, someone in a swim suit and goggles is climbing onto the stern and boarding the boat. I cannot imagine who would be coming out of Lake Michigan with these heavy waves and the boat in motion.

It is Ben Biddick (Bio, page 133), our boat captain and grinder who, unbeknown to me, had jumped off the side, dove under the boat and fastened a large rubber band around the folded propeller blades so that they do not cause extra drag as we make our way up the lake. This is called banding the prop. Although most racing boats have a propeller with blades which fold in together when the engine is not engaged, banding the blades is an extra precaution to prevent one or two blades from flopping around while the boat is under sail. PIED PIPER is probably one of few boats that band the prop, particularly on a day with 30 knots of breeze. Because I did not see Ben jump overboard, it sure is a shock to me. As he goes forward to the cabin to change clothes, Jack asks casually, "Are you alright, Ben?" To which Ben replies, "Fine."

It was ten years ago when my wife and I first saw a GL70. We had decided to drive up to Port Huron, Michigan for its annual "Boat Night" celebration. It was the Friday night before another Bayview Mackinac Race, which always went off on the following day. We parked behind some stores on the main street in town and were walking through a parking lot on our way to the Black River, which runs east to west through this port city.

This night, the river is host for hundreds of racing yachts filling its banks. We happened to arrive at a spot near the Port Huron Yacht Club, which is near the mouth of the river. In front of us were about eight very long and seemingly very narrow racing yachts. We had never seen anything like them before. Their great length combined with what appeared to be a narrow beam, prompted me to say that they looked like a knife. We were both amazed at what we had discovered and I wondered about the sailing skills, which were necessary to handle boats like these.

PIED PIPER crossing the finish line in 1987.

Impossible to imagine then, I would be racing aboard one of them ten years later.

How did the first Santa Cruz 70 happen to come to the Great Lakes? In 1985, Dick Jennings (Bio, page 148), (Jack's father) and his friend, John Rumsey were driving to Atlanta and talking about which boat best handles a downwind condition. John suggested the Santa Cruz 70 (SC70), designed and built in Santa Cruz, CA by naval architect, Bill Lee. He built it for racing in the annual Transpac Race from Los Angeles to Honolulu, a 2,200 mile distance. The first time he entered the race with this new design, Bill won. Dick flew out to California and saw hull #1, BLONDIE, built in 1983, which is now NITEMARE.

Dick thought the Chicago to Mackinac speed record established in 1911 could be broken with an SC70, but he did not share his idea with anyone. He built an SC70 in 1986, the fifth one ever built. In 1987, he broke the old speed record of 31 hours, 14 minutes with an elapsed time of 25 hours and 50 minutes. He had wind out of the southwest quadrant of 25 to 30 knots, which lasted for 24 hours. He was so early arriving to Mackinac Island that his crew made the lady's cocktail party held at the Grand Hotel at 4:00 p.m. Sunday. The Grand Hotel gave him the key for the whole crew and First National Bank of Chicago made a video of his race as a motivational tool. The bank also gave him a duplicate

Dick Jennings & crew celebrating a new speed record on the Chicago to Mackinac Race.

of the grandfather clock, which had been given to the owner of the
1911 winner, AMORITA. It was awarded to Dick by the grandson
of the owner of AMORITA. The seven foot clock stands in the
headquarters at Smithereen Pest Management Company.

Dick caused quite a stir on the Great Lakes with his SC70 and
was quickly followed by his friend, Bill Martin (Bio,page 164)
who bought STRIPES in 1988 and CYNOSURE, purchased
by Terry Kohler (Bio, page 154) in 1989. In 1995, they founded
the organization, known as the Great Lakes 70 Association and
changed the name from Santa Cruz 70 to Great Lakes 70 (GL70).

July 14, 2007, 2:20PM
START OF THE 2007 CHICAGO TO MACKINAC RACE
LATITUDE – 41 53.58N, LONGITUDE – 087 35.87W

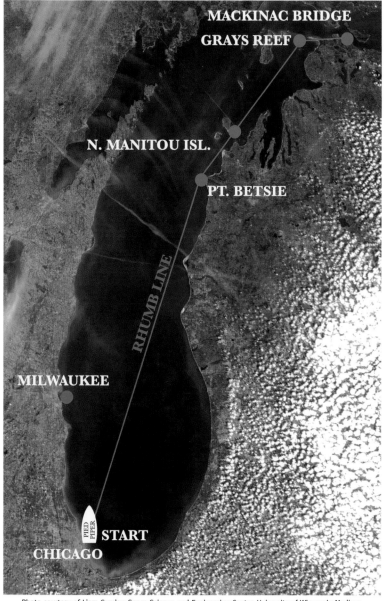

MACKINAC BRIDGE

GRAYS REEF

N. MANITOU ISL.

PT. BETSIE

RHUMB LINE

MILWAUKEE

PIED PIPER **START**

CHICAGO

Photo courtesy of Liam Gumley, Space Science and Engineering Center, University of Wisconsin-Madison.

We are in the countdown for the start of the GL70 Class close to the starting line along with EVOLUTION. Most of the others are further back, probably positioning themselves to build up more boat speed with a longer track. Every boat always wants to hit the line with clear air (no boats directly in front causing disturbed air behind them) on time, but not too early and with maximum speed.

Dave Jochum (Bio, page 140), the bowman, at his proper position for a start, is standing on the bow with one hand on the forestay and talking to the helmsman. Because of the distance between driver and bowman, Dave and Jack wear headsets to communicate with each other prior to the start. Dave talks through the start and doesn't use hand signals, which is the method used by most boats not equipped with the headsets. PIED PIPER is the only boat in the GL70 Class that does it this way. Jack wants to go off on the port end of the line. With very little time left, we make our turn for the spot we want. EVOLUTION sails to our right as we begin our approach. She tacks back and begins pointing for a spot very close to our destination. The cannon fires and a few seconds later we are across, ahead of all boats in our class. EVOLUTION crosses behind us and swings just aft of our stern on the way to getting clear air on our left. It is a great feeling to be first and moving fast. Although NITEMARE is a little late to the line at the start, she heads up the middle of the race course with boats to the right and left of her.

EVOLUTION wants to establish a position west of the fleet. They have analyzed two weather report sources prior to the start of the race and conclude that, although the race will begin with a strong southwesterly breeze, the wind will shift later in the day to a northerly breeze. The decisionmakers aboard do not anticipate that the winds will be above twenty knots. Because PIED PIPER performs better in a strong breeze than EVOLUTION, the heavier air actually experienced later in the day works to **PIED PIPER**'s advantage, allowing her to build and sustain a lead into the night.

The wind is still strong but has moved in a westerly direction and is now coming from our left and no longer behind us as we race northward. What a great feeling it is for everybody onboard! After months of planning, hours of hard work, meticulous crew selection and many days of practice sessions, we are on our way. The boat is moving well. Everyone possible is up on the windward rail hiking out, hoping with our weight to flatten the boat a little so that it can gain even more speed.

The angle of heel of a sailboat greatly affects her speed through the water. In heavy winds, crew weight is shifted as far out on the windward rail as possible. As the wind speed lightens, crew members are moved more amidships or even onto the leeward rail in very light air. Up on the rail, we have a great view of our competitors behind us. **EVOLUTION** seems to be going closer and closer to the Illinois shoreline with **MIRAGE** also behind and left of us. The rest of the fleet is either directly behind us or to our right.

After about three hours of racing, we can tell that the wind is slowing down and our boat speed with it. Although **EVOLUTION** and **MIRAGE** do not seem to be gaining on us, **NITEMARE**, off to our far right and seemingly in better air, begins to threaten our lead. We have a set of binoculars which, when focused on a competing boat in the distance, will show us the current position of the other boat in degrees. If, as an example, the other boat is at 240 degrees and one hour later is at 242 degrees, it is gaining on us. While watching **EVOLUTION** through the binoculars, it appears that we are maintaining our lead. **NITEMARE**, however, is a different story.

Another important piece of information about a competitor, is the type of headsail she is flying. All racing boats have numerous headsails, which are employed depending upon weather conditions and the angle of the wind in relation to the boat's heading (also known as point of sail). PIED PIPER carries two genoas, four jibs, including the storm jib, and five spinnakers. The jibs are identified by the numbers printed on the sail bag for each one and on the sail itself, so mistakes aren't made when hoisting. A #1 is the largest size jib and #2, #3 and #4 decrease in size proportionately. If you are replacing another size jib, you could hoist inside or outside the existing sail so that the boat does not lose speed during the exchange of one sail for another. The forestay contains two tracks which can accommodate two sails at a time.

Incorrect decisions on choice of a headsail can be very costly. This can be compounded by the amount of time required to retrieve the chosen replacement sail from down below, affix it to the forestay, fasten sheets (lines on the corner of the sail used for trimming) and hoist. If it appears that a sail change does not improve speed, the entire process must be reversed in order to return to your original or another configuration.

If you are replacing a spinnaker with a jib, you hoist the jib inside the spinnaker and lower it after the jib is up. The spinnaker is very large and holds a huge quantity of air in a heavy breeze. A spinnaker take down can be quite precarious if not done quickly. The sail can be blown overboard causing it to fill with water or remain filled with air aloft, causing the boat to have too much sail area exposed to the wind at one time. In extreme conditions, either of these situations could cause the boat to broach (heel over onto its side.)

There are two types of spinnakers in use. The symmetrical spinnaker has the head (top) of the sail lifted by a halyard (rope which raises and lowers the sail) to or near the top of the mast, leaving two corners equidistant on each side of the sail, each secured by a line running to the back of the boat on the port and starboard sides. Depending upon the direction of the wind, a large carbon fiber pole clamped onto a ring on the mast

GL70s racing together.

(spinnaker pole), will have its other end attached to one of the two corners of the sail and moved forward or backward depending on wind direction. The asymmetrical sail also has the head raised by the halyard, but one of the two remaining corners is affixed to a pole or the deck itself on or near the bow, which is stationary and does not move. The third corner has two sheets attached to it, each running down opposite sides of the boat.

A very effective technique used to bring a loaded spinnaker down quickly is called the "letterbox takedown." It involves taking the (unused) spinnaker sheet not currently under a load and pulling it into the opening between the bottom (foot) of the mainsail and the boom. Once the halyard of the spinnaker is loosened, crew members begin pulling the spinnaker down and through this opening straight down into the main companionway leading to the cabin below. As the sail passes through the "letterbox," it flattens out, loses its air and is easily stuffed into the cabin, taking it out of the wind and off the deck. This process is expedited even more quickly with the help of the pit man down in the cabin, pulling the sail straight down, thus not allowing it to re-inflate in the distance between the boom and the top of the hatch. Of course, the entire cabin is now filled with this enormous sail which must be repacked properly for the next hoist. Although space is more cramped down below than on the deck, the sail is out of the wind and the repacking process is made much more manageable.

Jack demonstrating proper use of a crossover chart.

Sometimes, in the same wind conditions, a competitor will change its headsail and gain speed on you. You must always be vigilant and watch those boats in sight to see how they're doing and which headsails they're flying. If another boat changes to a new headsail and finds it was the wrong decision, you can watch them and see if it would possibly be a mistake for you to use the same size sail. If, however, in the same air, a competitor changes headsails, which perform better than your present choice, a quick sail change may be warranted.

PIED PIPER is using a crossover chart which Jack has developed. It is a matrix with the two variables; true wind speed and true wind angle. Both measurements are fairly reliable on its OCKAM system, which uses sensors and a sophisticated computer system to determine true wind speed and true wind angle. These measurements differ with apparent wind speed and apparent wind angle. True wind measurements exclude the movement and heading of the boat. Apparent wind measurements include boat speed and direction. This takes the guess work out of choosing sail setup.

In order to make the right decision, you can't guess. You have to know what will work and the crossover chart is a record of what has worked in the past. In most high level professional programs (such as the Volvo Ocean Race), two boat testing is used to create the crossover chart. Since two boat testing is not possible in our situation, head-to-head racing in the class has been used through trial and error to constantly tweak the entries in the chart.

Throughout the summer of 2007, there were three different versions of the chart based upon racing experiences. Creating a chart like this can be very helpful because, in the GL70 class, every

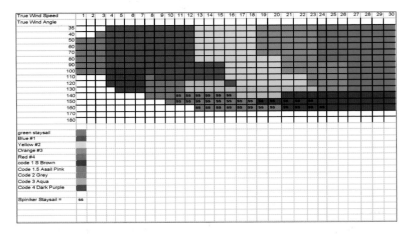

boat and sail is designed a little differently. The above chart shows, as an example, if the True Wind Speed is 15 knots and the True Wind Angle is 90 degrees, the #1 (Blue #1) jib should be flown.

At the start of the Chicago Mac Race, PIED PIPER chose a #3 jib, while NITEMARE chose a sail called a blast reacher. In PIED PIPER's development of a sail inventory, Jack felt that a blast reacher had a very small window of effective use on a GL70. Jack concluded that the cost of the sail outweighed its usefulness. These types of decisions are made at the discretion of each boat owner. Instead of choosing a reacher, he built his #2 genoa with a higher clew. This is a compromise to upwind performance because he is sacrificing end-plate effect, but it makes the sail more effective while reaching.

One of the dreaded moments in racing is now possibly upon us. There is nothing more painful than to work for and attain a lead, only to see it evaporate when another boat, under worse or identical weather conditions, begins to rein you in. The sun is going down and the wind from the west has slowed considerably. We can see NITEMARE and its shiny red hull has drawn even with us. She is still far off to starboard as we all continue north. Eventually, it appears that she takes the lead for a while. The crew members aboard NITEMARE see that they've taken the lead and feel good that they have accomplished this despite their late start.

Yacht races are not only about sail inventory, crew capabilities and great steering; they are also about where your boat is located in relation to what is happening in the ever-fickle, always-changing weather pattern. After seeming helpless while watching NITEMARE advance, we get a little increase in wind speed and, aided by a favorable wind shift, take off, crossing NITEMARE's bow and moving back into the lead. It seems for hours afterward we continue to extend it every minute. NITEMARE and the rest of the fleet stall off Racine, WI. PIED PIPER and EVOLUTION move off together because they pick up a breeze closer to shore.

Later, as the wind builds up in strength once again, it also shifts to the north. Now, the pounding begins. PIED PIPER is taking the ever-increasing waves on the nose. The boat is moving well and the large waves confronting us have good momentum too. Every time the bow hits a new wave, the 68' boat shudders. Every crewman feels each and every impact. By this time, the sun is going down quickly. It is getting colder and those of us on the rail near the mast, are getting intermittent spray. Shortly thereafter, each man goes below and changes into foul weather gear and multiple layers of clothing. The Chicago skyline, which I had been watching throughout the afternoon, is now out of sight.

Bob Wiesen is performing one of the greatest juggling acts I have ever witnessed. With the boat rocking and pitching as it crashes through each wave, he is preparing dinner below in the galley. I have gone down to change and come upon him and his awesome performance. He has about eight bowls on the counter, which is constantly in motion. Each one is being loaded with macaroni and then placed on a larger paper plate with pieces of fried chicken. It is obvious that Bob, in his many years of sailing distance races, has learned something about the dynamics of a boat underway in heavy seas. Not one spec of food is spilled during the entire preparation process. Once loaded, each plate is handed up to someone on deck and the food is quickly distributed. We have been long enough into the race by now that, until we reach Grays Reef on the edge of the Mackinac Straits, someone is almost always asleep in one of the twelve bunks in the crew's quarters below. PIED PIPER's bunks are all adjusted to the boat's angle of heel, thus allowing a person at rest to remain level.

Jack remembers the start of the race in his own words:

"This was the first Chicago Mackinac Race that I have skippered which had a good breeze at the start. I was happy about this as our boat performs very well in any conditions above 10 knots of wind speed. I was also very confident in our crew's ability to handle the conditions and the boat better than our competitors. Leading up to the start, we were considering the #4 or #3 jib, although we were all really hoping that the wind would shift to the left far enough for a spinnaker. This, however, was not to be because the course off the starting line was a close reach. The start of a distance race is not that important other than, if you nail the start, you get a good morale boost and can start executing your long term strategy without any other boats dictating your tactics.

We reached into the starting area with the #3 and a full main and started to assess the starting line. Our long term strategy was to get as far north as fast as possible. This meant we wanted to start at the weather end of the line on port tack. If that end of the line looked too crowded, we also considered approaching on starboard and using that right of way to get the spot at the left end of the line, then tacking to port and heading up the lake. While on starboard tack, we headed back towards the starting line and saw where our competitors had lined up to make their final approaches. The left end of the line was fairly clear of other boats. This made our job easier to make a timed run to the point on the line where we wanted to start.

Perry Lewis at the helm.

Perry Lewis (Bio, page 142) and I were working the time and distance, with Mike Hoey (Bio, page 139) trimming the main. In the strong breeze it was hard to hear one another. This caused us to execute our final tack to the line about 30 seconds earlier than we had wanted. We sailed at half speed to burn the time and eventually, with about 45 seconds left, trimmed the sails and headed for the line. It was a good start and the best of our class. We could have done better because we were about a half a boat length late. We rolled over the top of EVOLUTION and were able to head to our course of 15 to 20 degrees with no interference from any other boats. The start was a success."

In the harbor that morning, Jack had conducted the usual pre-race crew meeting. In addition to verifying each man's starting position and the latest weather report, he announced that Mike Hoey and Perry Lewis would be the two watch captains. The thirteen-man crew would be split into two six-man watches, A and B, with Jack floating on his own schedule. Each watch was to be

Mike Hoey at the helm.

three hours in length, with half the crew on deck and the other
half resting or sleeping below. The exceptions to this rule were
at the discretion of the skipper. If he wanted to make a headsail
change as an example, he might decide to wake up Dave Jochum,
the bowman, to get on deck and take the responsibility for making
it happen. When a crewman goes below to sleep, he is expected
to select a bunk which is on the windward side of the boat so that,
even while asleep, his weight is helping the boat go fast.

Another crew member, Mike Hoey has been a professional sailor
for many years. In 2007, he and his partners won the U.S. National
Match Racing Championship. These are his observations about
the GL70s and the PIED PIPER Racing Program:

1. The GL70 is the only 70 foot one-design class in the world.
2. Competitive sailing's true sailing foundation is in one-design. Pure one-design! Free of design difference.
3. The TP 52 is a talented group but is not one-design because each new boat makes the others obsolete.
4. Just build one-design of boat and only change deck hardware, etc.

Terry Kohler at the helm of EVOLUTION.

5. Jack has a lot of good people. They can change sails faster than others.
6. Jack's guys are dinghy sailors and can do any job on the boat.
7. NITEMARE and EVOLUTION will be big competitors on the Mackinac Races.
8. In most MAC Races, midnight to 6:00 a.m. is the money watch. You must remain alert and be ready and willing to make a 3:00 a.m. sail change in the rain.
9. Mike personally recommended that Jack choose Detroit guys because there are many more races conducted on Lake St. Clair than in the Chicago area and these young guys come to the boat with a lot of racing experience.
10. Key growth in any sailing program is in exposing drivers and crew to new teachers/tacticians who can spur growth in new directions.

In terms of safety, Mike believes that PIED PIPER is well prepared. He feels that this boat is better equipped than the race

BLOW 'EM TO SMITHEREENS on the hard in Muskegon.

committee boat. As a paramedic, he brings a defibrillator and medicine kit aboard, which includes various medicines, bandages and suturing tools. The boat has two EPIRBs (Emergency Position Indicating Radio Beacon), flares, parachute rockets, personal flotation devices (PFD), harnesses and tethers.

He also believes a good man overboard (MOB) drill should be conducted in a pool while wearing all foul weather gear and layered clothing to see if the PFD can sustain the crewman and the extra weight of wet clothing. His premise is that wearing a PFD may not save someone's life if its flotation is inadequate for a specific person's weight including all wet clothing. It becomes more critical, when racing in a Mackinac Race, with the cold temperature of the water in northern Lake Michigan and Lake Huron. Mike feels it would take on average twenty-five minutes to pick up a man overboard. This assumes that someone on deck keeps the person in sight and that there is an adequate number of crewmen awake and alert enough to immediately render assistance.

Perry Lewis, the other watch captain, has had vast international racing experience and has won the Mackinac race in class many times. He is a sail maker with North Sails. As I returned to the deck, the wind and waves are still out of the north and the helmsman is pushing the boat as fast as he can. I find a spot on the windward rail next to Mike Hoey. He explains that this particular hull has water tight bulkheads, which make it stiffer when sailing upwind. So, the heavy wind on the nose is an advantage for PIED PIPER. I tell him I am prepared to take this pounding all the way to the finish if it will help us win the race. I really didn't think we would travel this far north along the Wisconsin shoreline before crossing over to the Michigan side.

As it grows dark, after approximately six hours, the wind begins to slow once again. We have definitely put more distance between us and EVOLUTION during the heavy weather. However, as we approach Milwaukee we can see her creeping up on our port stern. It becomes apparent to me that the crew aboard EVOLUTION is going to be hard to beat.

EVOLUTION is owned by Terry Kohler, who also owns North Sails. He is a veteran racer with over forty years of experience. Of all the choices he has in the yacht racing world, none can top his love of racing the sleds (as these boats are sometimes called) to Mackinac Island.

Peter Reichelsdorfer (Bio, page 156) is a co-skipper with Terry aboard EVOLUTION. Pete has two sons who work for Windway Corporation, the holding company of a number of Kohler-owned companies. Pete is Director of Corporate Liaison, North Marine Group. His two sons and two daughters race with him aboard EVOLUTION. His son, Dan (Bio, page 157), is also a co-skipper and boat captain. They also have four friends who are both regular crewmembers and employees of Harken, a major supplier of marine hardware.

Pete's comments about racing the GL70:

1. "It's big, but not huge; very fast off the wind.
2. Sticky upwind in light air.
3. During buoy racing, loads and gears are not too hard to handle.
4. The boat allows us to sail with a crew not needing extensive experience.
5. The GL70 is not overpowering or quirky.
6. It's a great all around boat!"

In early June of 2007, Dick Jennings came out of sailing retirement and bought a GL70 called COLT 45 from one

The above photo was taken at the Park Grille party. Dick Jennings is in the white shirt in the front row.

of the association's owners. His primary motive was to keep another GL70 in the Great Lakes. He also had another idea in mind. The 2007 Chicago to Mackinac Race would be the twentieth anniversary of his record-breaking achievement in the 1987 race. He decided to invite all his former crewmembers from the '87 race to join him aboard this boat for this year's race. Eight of them accepted his invitation.

Since COLT 45 had not been raced since 2005, when it won both Mackinac Races, there was plenty of work to do in the brief time remaining. Upon the closing of the purchase, Dick went up to Muskegon, MI where the boat was stored at Torreson Marine and immediately put a refurbishing plan together. He also renamed the boat, "BLOW EM TO SMITHEREENS," alluding to the name of his company.

On Thursday, July 12, two days before the 2007 Chicago Race, Dick hosted a great party at the Park Grille in downtown Chicago for all past and present PIED PIPER crew members. Each of the original crew was given a polo shirt commemorating the date of the 1987 victory and its record-breaking time. Every attendee was also given an autographed chart of Lake Michigan showing the precise position of the boat as it reached significant landmarks along the race course.

MEET THE BOAT & CREW
BLOW 'EM TO SMITHEREENS USA 50045

BLOW 'EM TO SMITHEREENS during a pre-race practice.

20th Anniversary Crew aboard BLOW 'EM TO SMITHEREENS.

Jamie Schwarz.......................... Livingston , MT
Paul Snow .... Lake Forest, IL
J B Kuppe................................ Palo Alto, CA
Alex Dansberger...................... Minneapolis, MN
Tom Fink................................. Washington , DC
Bob Stumpf .... Vernon Hills , IL
Tom Abood............................. Minneapolis, MN
Lars Hansen............................ Golden Valley, MN
Bill Wagner .... Milwaukie , OR
Dick Jennings .... Niles , IL
Bob Kiehl................................ Akron, OH
Bill Willman .... Milwaukee, WI
John Bosco .... Chicago, IL
Sean Wagner........................... Milwaukie, OR

OFF OF MILWAUKEE
JULY 14, 2007-11:37 PM
LATITUDE – 43 03.963N, LONGITUDE – 087 26.471W
COG (Course over ground): 37 DEGREES,
SOG (Speed over ground): 9.3 knots

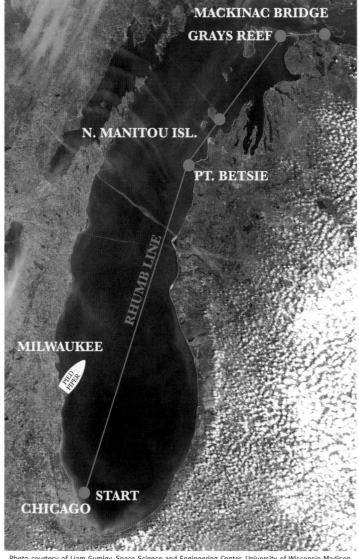

Photo courtesy of Liam Gumley, Space Science and Engineering Center, University of Wisconsin-Madison.

Off Milwaukee at sunset.

After the huge breeze at the start of the race and subsequent strong and weak weather cells experienced throughout Saturday afternoon and evening, it is still the same day and we're off downtown Milwaukee at 11:30 p.m. and showing a Speed Over Ground (SOG) reading on the GPS of 9.3 knots. As we look aft and towards the Wisconsin shoreline on our left, we see that EVOLUTION continues to shadow us. It seems their strategy is to hug the shoreline in the hope that they might pick up some thermal breezes not available to our position further out in the lake. Nonetheless, they do not gain on us during this period of time. The crew aboard EVOLUTION feels they are well positioned off Milwaukee Saturday night. She is the second place boat on the water and remains on starboard while stretching out into the lake.

I can't believe I am off shore at night and looking at the familiar Milwaukee skyline once again. Just two weeks prior, at the invitation of Sam Nedeau (Bio, page 169), I raced from Muskegon, Michigan to Milwaukee aboard another GL70, WINDANCER,

Dave Jochum switching spinnakers while underway.

and raced back two nights later in the 69th sailing of the Queen's
Cup Race. Although I had never sailed on Lake Michigan
before, I would cover over 500 miles on this beautiful lake in
three separate distance races between June 27th and July 16th.

Later that night, the wind slackens to about three knots. This is
not unusual. Night or day, these racing crews never take their eyes
off the continuous objective of maximum boat speed. How do
you make a 25,000 pound, 68-foot boat maximize its speed with

three knots of wind? One of the ironies
about the GL70 is that it can actually be
made to exceed wind speed with the right
sails and good trimmers. The photo on
the left shows the readings aboard the
GL70 WINDANCER in an earlier race.
The top reading of 4.44 knots is boat
speed compared to wind speed shown in

Dave Shriner tuning the rig while underway.

the middle instrument of 3.5 knots. In this example, the boat is actually traveling almost one knot faster than the speed of the wind itself. This phenomenon is the result of many of the dynamics built into these boats, including such factors as mast height, sail sizes, hull shape and boat weight. So, in very light air, when most boats are standing still, a GL70 can move away from the fleet.

Early in the morning around 1:00 a.m., we begin hearing a rattling sound high up in the rig. It is noticeable because there should not be such a sound if the rig is tuned properly. Ben Biddick is involved in the discussion and, with input from a couple of the other guys, decides that one of the diagonal supports (referred to as a D, such as D3) has come loose during the heavy pounding the boat endured earlier. These diagonals run from the mast connection of one spreader to the outside tip of the spreader beneath it. Because the mast is so high above the deck (approx. 78'), the diagonals play the important role of providing extra strength to the mast when under heavy loads. The adjustment of these diagonals is usually done by Dave Shriner (Bio, page 145) (photo on page 41), a professional rigger.

At this time, however, Dave is sleeping down below and the decision was made not to wake him. So, Ben is hoisted up the mast with tools in hand. Whenever a crewman is hoisted, two halyards are attached to a bosun's chair he wears around his waist and under his thighs. While Ben is tightening the diagonal, someone on deck is looking up the mast to make sure that it is straight. He is not lowered until the amount of new tension on the diagonal seems to be correct. In this case, it takes about fifteen minutes.

A light air situation can often provide the opportunity to sneak away on an opponent. It is even better if that opportunity comes in total darkness. Although the city lights up the sky to a certain degree, the distance between us and EVOLUTION can be lengthened if we make the right sail decisions and trim them effectively. Jack goes back to his crossover chart to see which combination of headsails will work best in these conditions.

When the decision is made for a sail change, people are mobilized immediately whether previously awake or asleep. Very seldom are sail changes made "bare headed" (without the existing sail remaining aloft until the replacement has been hoisted).

For this change, Jack asks that Dave Jochum, our bowman, be awakened and come topside in order to gather his foredeck crew together for the exchange of sails.

The photo on page 40 shows Dave in an earlier practice session swapping out spinnakers while being suspended about twenty feet above the water and ten feet off the starboard side of the boat. Earlier, during a pre-race practice session, while suspended high above the boat, he threw his shoulder out of its socket. Despite the incredible pain, he had pushed it back in place before being lowered to the deck.

The foredeck crew for this race consists of Dave at the bow, J.B Schumaker (Bio, page 144) at mid bow, Brian Brophy (Bio, page 136) on mast and Eric Jochum (Bio, page 141), Dave's younger brother, on halyards. Jack calls for a certain sail to be brought on deck from the cabin. Eric and J.B. run down and retrieve the sail. Because of the size of these boats, everything is much larger than on most boats. This is especially true of the sail sizes. Each one is kept in a blue bag with a zipper running the full length. The bags are about thirty feet long and are unwieldy and heavy. The sail is dragged to the bow and unzipped so it may be attached to the headstay. Two sheets are attached to the clew so that it may be trimmed when flying. The order is given to hoist and Brian begins jumping the halyard (jumping into the air to use his body weight as extra leverage when pulling on the halyard to raise the replacement sail.) Eric takes up the slack of the halyard as it goes around the winch. They work together as a team very well and the many sail changes made in this long distance race are performed with great expediency.

At night, with three hour shifts, the change from one watch to another is an important factor. Some people are more awake and alert than others. As we proceed further north in the Lake Michigan, the air becomes much colder. Add in one other ingredient, dew at night on the deck and deck hardware, and you have a rather miserable set of circumstances. Nevertheless, when the members of a watch are awakened and sent topside, everyone is expected to perform properly. Luckily, on this night we do not have fog as another complicating factor.

Why would anyone want to put themselves in such a situation? I believe most racing sailors would include the following motives:

1. They love to compete in a very exhilarating sport against great competitors. In addition to being a physical challenge, it's also a great chess game and very mentally stimulating. For most, if not all, of the GL 70 racers the fun is the racing itself, not

necessarily the experience of sailing. Very few of them ever go "for a sail." My daughter, Sarah, asked Jack if after the racing season he ever took the big boat out for an afternoon of sailing. His response was, "What's the point?" I rest my case.

2. Sailing is a true adventure because there are always so many unknown elements. Every race is completely different than any other. Everything changes including weather, competitors, tactics, potential equipment failures and/or crew errors in judgment or execution. Will we confront heavy weather and, if so, will we be able to handle it successfully? Unlike any other sport, the playing field, or in our case, the race course is never the same from one hour to the next. We are always racing on a constantly changing surface with varying wind speeds and directions. Our course for this race, Lake Michigan, is roughly 70 NM wide and 300NM long. That's a big race course. Regardless of which circumstances develop, you can't make a quick exit. In the Indy 500, you can always pull into the pits. Not so, out here; not when you are thirty miles from any landfall.

3. You must depend upon one another. Thirteen to fifteen people live in a constantly moving boat, frequently under adverse conditions. Day and night, some are coming on or going off watch, people are sleeping, eating, working, discussing strategy, observing competitors and obtaining weather and other information from the navigation station. Decisions are always being made on tactics, weight placement, sail trim and a myriad of other things, all of which affect boat speed and performance. Despite the large size of a GL70 on deck and in the cabin, it is still close quarters for such a big crew. Everyone must show patience so there is not a breakdown in morale. Despite the individual needs of any crewman, focus must always be on helping the boat go fast. Also, a crew member could become sick or injured. In this event, other

PIED PIPER and EVOLUTION at sunset.

crew members must be aware of his condition and needs. Someone could be designated as the primary person to assist the sick or injured man. In our case we had Mike Hoey, a certified paramedic, onboard. It is highly unusual on most boats, but not a GL70, to have a crew member with Mike's medical credentials. A couple of the guys did seek a little medical attention from Mike during the race. In closing this discussion about depending upon one another, it must be noted that there is usually tremendous camaraderie among a racing crew. Everyone wants to be there and has probably expended great effort to re-arrange business and personal commitments in order to take time out each summer for these distance races. We all share a common fate. We win or lose together. We endure hardship and the expenditure of effort and sacrifice for our common goal of success. As you "ride the rail" with sailors packed shoulder-to-shoulder for hours at a time, you learn about their lives and character.

45

Also, when you're "out there" in open water on a night watch, there is a shared experience which is difficult to describe, but, nonetheless, very meaningful. From time-to-time you also see acts of personal courage and a complete abandonment of self for the well being of the crew and its mission.

4. Distance racing is particularly exciting. In a distance race such as this one, you step off the dock in Chicago and step onto the dock on Mackinac Island, having traversed the entire distance by wind, water and boat. So, it is not only a race. It is a long journey over hundreds of miles of open water, far offshore day and night.

On the Chicago to Mackinac Race, there are many sights. Sunsets and sunrises are incredible. It visually appears that the fiery ball is either sinking into or rising from the lake itself. The city of Chicago also provides an awesome backdrop for the start and can be seen for many hours out in the lake as we move northward.

Although, only two of the five GL70 events are long distance Mackinac Races, these are the most important to all the racers. The morning of the race, cars filled with sailors and their loved ones fill Chicago's Lakeshore Drive as they drive by the various harbors in search of the one where a certain boat is moored. Some family members may accompany their sailor, with sea bag in tow, down to the boat itself for a final goodbye and greeting to the other crew members already onboard. Others execute the farewell rituals at the car with the family headed in one direction and the sailor in another.

While we were waiting in the van for one of our guys to grab his gear off another boat, I noticed a big guy getting out of his car. He picked up the sea bag, kissed his wife goodbye, handed her the bag, got back in the car and drove away. She threw the bag over her shoulder and began walking down to her boat. Many of the boats have female crew members and there are boats, which are owned and skippered by female sailors. Two days later, some of these families make the long drive out of Chicago, through northern Indiana and up the entire length of the state of Michigan to Mackinac Island so they can be on hand when the boats and their crews arrive in the harbor.

It is now about 1:00 a.m. on Sunday morning. I have been awake since 6:00 a.m. Saturday morning and have decided not to go below on the shift changes with my watch. I know this is a once-in-a-lifetime opportunity for me and I don't want to miss a thing. I figure that after the race is over I will have plenty of time to catch up on my sleep. Any sailor would tell you that I am not doing the right thing and they would be correct. I should use the opportunities for sleep when they are available.

I am sitting on the starboard rail with my tether attached to the lifeline. Because the wind has died down, Jack wants to shift the crew weight to leeward. So, those of us on deck move over to the port side. As I look at him at the helm, my mind goes back to the discussion we had on Friday morning.

Before our last pre-race practice that morning, I had an opportunity to talk to Jack alone in the kitchen of his house in Lincoln Park. I was sure that he felt under a lot of pressure. The big day was just around the corner. A large sum of money had been spent in the off season on new sails and he, Ben and J.B. had put many hours of work into boat preparation. He had meticulously assembled a very talented crew who would expect good leadership from the skipper. Mike Hoey and Perry Lewis were veteran racers and would be consulted throughout the long race. The skippers and crews of the other nine GL70s were some of the best racers in the Great Lakes and throughout the country. They had sailed the Chicago Race three and four times as often as Jack and knew the nuances of the lake and its varying weather patterns. Many of this year's crew sailed with him on the Chicago Mackinac Race last year. They were upset about its outcome, considering they were leading the entire fleet at the outset. He would be racing against his dad for the first time in his life and comparisons would be made. And to top it all off, he would have this guy on the boat watching his every move and recording it in a book yet to be written. That's a handful.

We sat down and talked. In addition to my appreciation for his invitation to race on PIED PIPER, I had grown to admire him and his serious efforts to bring both boat and crew up to the level needed to compete in the GL70 Class. I felt he showed strong leadership traits for a young man twenty-seven years old. I finished my remarks by saying, "We are all behind you. You have done all you can to prepare the boat and all of us. Everything is ready. Now, you deserve to have fun and enjoy this race." He told me he appreciated it and we had a great final practice day.

The boat begins to move again and the lights of Milwaukee are beginning to fade in the distance. The decks are usually wet with dew at night unless the winds are strong enough to keep the boat's surface dry. They are not strong enough on this night. Although we are a good distance offshore, I can see a few lights here and there on the Wisconsin shore. It is obvious we are not attempting to get over to the Michigan shore at this point. We just continue our progress northward.

Jack recalls making our way up to Milwaukee on Saturday night: "EVOLUTION and MIRAGE had worked their way to the left of us and the wind had shifted to the right so now all the boats had tacked to starboard. We maintained a loose cover on EVOLUTION as they continued to try and foot out to get leverage to the left of us. We continued with this situation until after dark. We knew we were going to have to tack to port eventually. We just didn't want to allow anyone near us to gain significant leverage to our left.

It became apparent that EVOLUTION was waiting for us to tack so they could have a clear lane on our hip to sail in. This was alright with me as it was a little too early in the race to make it into a full on match race between the two boats. The port tack was quickly becoming favored. So, we tacked to port and kept an eye on EVOLUTION which followed shortly afterwards. I remember that driving the boat during this time of the race was very difficult as there was a pretty good wave chop right on the nose. Perry Lewis had a good touch on the helm during this time period and helped keep the boat moving. After we tacked to port, everyone was pushing really hard to keep the boat going fast, even to the point where we were getting a little short with each other when the boat speed would drop even a tenth of a knot for any period of time. This situation with the crew was the result of a little bit of fatigue setting in and the fact that the team really wanted to do well and extend our lead."

MEET THE BOAT & CREW
STRIPES USA 25168

One of the boats trailing us is STRIPES which is owned by Bill Martin (Bio, page 164) and was, as mentioned earlier, the second SC70 which came to the Great Lakes.

STRIPES sailing by the Grand Hotel on Mackinac island

STRIPES Crew List – 2007 Chicago to Mackinac Race

John Teeter........................ Ann Arbor, MI
J.D. Turbitt .... Owen Sound, Ontario
Seth Martin........................ Chicago, IL
Stu Pettitt .... Grosse Pointe Park, MI
Bill & Sally Martin............ Ann Arbor, MI`
Jack Morman .... Harrison Township, MI
Tim LaBute....................... Windsor, Ontario, Canada, N8S 4R1
Mike Martin....................... Ann Arbor, MI
Chris Woodall .... Windsor, Ontario, Canada , N8W
John Johns .... Ann Arbor, MI
Bill Bird............................. Washington, DC
Dave Lyons .... Palo Alto, CA
Dan Knight........................ Chicago, IL

JULY 15, 2007-4:07 PM
OFF POINT BETSIE LIGHT
LATITUDE – 44 41.376N, LONGITUDE – 086 21.081W
COG: 56 DEGREES, SOG: 8.4 KNOTS

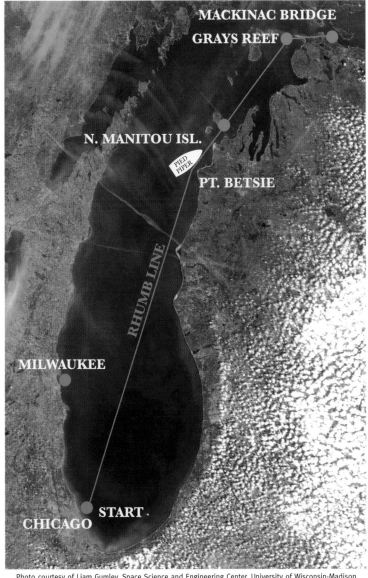

MACKINAC BRIDGE
GRAYS REEF
N. MANITOU ISL.
PIED PIPER
PT. BETSIE
RHUMB LINE
MILWAUKEE
START
CHICAGO

Photo courtesy of Liam Gumley, Space Science and Engineering Center, University of Wisconsin-Madison.

Pointe Betsie Light. Photo courtesy of WalkSoftlyPhotos.com.

We emerge from the Wisconsin shore shortly after daybreak and begin moving in a northeasterly direction across the middle of the lake toward the Michigan shore. The next significant landmark will be the Point Betsie Light, located on a part of the Michigan shoreline that juts out into the lake. It is south of the well-known and very distinctive Sleeping Bear Sand Dune.

On Sunday morning, EVOLUTION is close to a line extending between Sheboygan, Wisconsin and Pentwater, Michigan. She is still in second place and about two miles behind PIED PIPER. Obviously, the crew members are veterans of many, many Chicago to Mackinac races. Their experiences over the years have led them to a number of conclusions which guide their thinking in each subsequent race. One of their major conclusions is the thought that if they are among the top four boats on Sunday morning, they have an excellent chance of being very competitive and will be a contender for a first place finish.

Sam Nedeau, a co-skipper with his dad aboard WINDANCER, has said that these distance races have an accordion effect. All the boats seem to be spread out over great distances and periodically come together. The accordion is definitely at work today. Although, we still have a substantial lead, we can see a number of boats behind us. It seems that EVOLUTION is still keeping pace with us when about midday the breeze falls off once again. EVOLUTION remains far off to our left while NITEMARE is making a bid to gain on us by coming up much closer to the Michigan Shore on our right. These are the two closest challengers at this point. Others are in sight directly behind us, but at a considerable distance behind the two challengers. When the boats are so spread out, one or two might happen to be in a favorable weather pattern with a stronger breeze than others. This could allow them to surpass the leader in a matter of minutes if the leader is not so favored. Conversely, the leader could be in better air, allowing for a substantial gain on all comers.

None of these possible scenarios happen on Sunday afternoon. It is basically a stalemate despite the great effort on our boat to find a sliver of air we can use for our escape. All the crewmen around me, although frustrated with the light air conditions, have obviously been in this situation many times throughout their sailing careers. It is, however, hard to believe that you can be in the middle of such an immense body of water and feel hardly a whisper of air.

Patience & Perseverance

Sailors say that you just have to take whatever Mother Nature gives and make the best of it. Likewise, we all must take what life has to offer and make the best of it. In fact, I believe there are many life lessons to be learned and re-learned aboard a sailboat during a long distance race. Two of the most necessary personal qualities would be patience and perseverance.

Patience: As mentioned earlier, there is no quick escape from undesirable circumstances. You are thirty miles offshore with no wind, a scorching sun and huge biting flies which materialize out of nowhere. You send someone up the rig to look for a hint of a breeze coming from any direction, but he reports nothing in sight. So, you sit and try to keep covered up to protect you from the sun and the flies. Or you may be in the rear of the fleet with the same weather conditions plus the knowledge that it is very unlikely you will be able to substantially improve your position on the leaders far ahead.

Conversely, you can be caught in the height of a relentless storm, which shows no signs of letting up. After you have consulted any available weather predictions in the navigation station, decided on the ideal sail trim, crew weight adjustments and boat heading, you must accept your fate and make the best of it.

It doesn't matter how large the boat happens to be. Little irritations among the crew are unavoidable. When crew members are thrown together for long periods of time, often in frustrating circumstances, frictions can arise. These frictions, if verbalized, can have a harmful affect on crew morale. Also it is not unusual for a big boat, with a crew of fifteen people, to embark on a distance race with four or five members who are complete strangers to the others. So you learn about one another as the race progresses. However, you all know that because you share a common fate, the successful completion of the race and the personal safety of one another depends upon good cooperation and effective teamwork.

You must also be patient with the skipper of the boat. You are aboard as a result of his or her personal invitation. Someone has to be in charge and allowed to be the final decision-maker. All skippers have their own style of communication and decision-making. Some prefer to seek the advice of other crew members while others rely solely on their instincts and experience to decide. Whatever the style or personality quirks he or she may have, the skipper is still the skipper.

There is one situation, however, which is an exception to this tradition. For some skippers, success in the race takes precedence over boat and crew safety. This is not unusual aboard racing yachts. Certain skippers get a reputation in this regard. It is, however, understood that some element of risk is usually acceptable by the crew in order to win. After all, this is yacht racing. Even with a cautious skipper, there are a number of means by which a crewmember could be injured or killed. All racing sailors accept these realities as part of their decision to participate in the sport. There is a point, however, when the crew knows the degree of risk is unacceptable and downright dangerous. When this point is reached, some will usually speak up.

I think I would be remiss if I didn't comment on the PIED PIPER's crewmembers and their acceptance of having me onboard. Although, I admitted upfront that I did not possess their highly developed sailing skills, I'm sure it became equally obvious watching me in action. Jack had through a meticulous process

PIED PIPER with Sleeping Bear Sand Dunes off the port bow.

that took over four years, assembled a tremendous crew of highly skilled sailors, each one specializing in a certain requirement needed to maximize the power of a GL70. One of the attractions for these guys was the opportunity to race alongside other great sailors aboard **PIED PIPER**. Then, for the Chicago Mackinac Race, Jack invites an unqualified, sixty-five-year-old sailor with limited skills and distance racing experience. I think they liked the idea of having a book written about them. More importantly, however, they wanted to win the race. So was this guy going to be a liability onboard and if so, how much of a liability? Hopefully, during the four days we practiced out in Lake Michigan in front of that great Chicago skyline, they realized that I conducted myself safely around the boat and didn't attempt to do anything someone else should be doing. In any event, I will always be grateful for their kindness and camaraderie displayed repeatedly in each practice session and throughout the race.

Dave Shriner (on the left) at the helm with Ben Biddick, Mike Hoey and Jack Jennings.

Perseverance: Especially during a long distance race, perseverance is a necessary attribute of everyone aboard. For example, the Chicago to Mackinac Race is approximately 290 NM in length. Depending upon weather conditions and the length of the boat, a crew could be out there between thirty and seventy hours. The GL70 fleet usually completes the course in thirty to fifty hours, much sooner than all the boats shorter in length. Everyone onboard looks forward to this once-a-year event. Of course, the skippers expend the most money, personal time and effort to prepare the boat and recruit a competitive crew. Each crew member and his or her family also make sacrifices so they can take time away to practice and participate in the race. Many crewmembers also adhere to a physical workout program so they can handle the requirements of their position on the boat. One of the positions on a GL70 requiring the most physical strength and good cardio conditioning is that of grinder. Because the primary winches, used to trim the headsails, are so large and heavy, a device called a grinder is used to trim them when under a load. It is mounted on the deck half way between the port and starboard primary winches. It has pedals or handles which resemble the pedals of a bicycle connected under the deck to each winch. When the order is given to trim a jib or spinnaker, the grinder, with a hand on each pedal, begins turning the grinder at a higher and higher rate of speed. This continues until the trimmer says to stop. It is physically exhausting and usually done by certain crewmembers who specialize in it. In our case, Ben Biddick is the grinder.

The bow position is also physically demanding as well as one of the most dangerous jobs on the boat. Dave Jochum, the bowman on PIED PIPER, is in tremendous physical shape, as is his brother Eric, who is on halyards. Mid bow is a position not seen on many boats, but necessary on a GL70. This position is between that of the bowman and the mast. J.B. Schumaker is mid bow and has the duel role of helping Eric retrieve sails from down below and assist Dave in preparing the sails for hoisting.

Because of all the preparation by everyone onboard, all crew members have an obligation to do whatever they can at every moment to help the boat win. This is a tall order considering that each person is expected to perform at his or her best for two days and nights under a variety of weather conditions and racing circumstances. Night time is most difficult. You are sleeping three hours and working three hours and climbing out of a warm bunk and emerging on deck where it is cold, wet and dark. The boat is alive and moving at max speed. The on-deck crew expect you to acclimate yourself quickly with all the things you need to know in order to continue the boat's present momentum. For example, you could come up in the midst of a sail change or a tack or jibe. Because you emerge from the cabin directly in the center of the boat and under the boom,

you have to be aware that a turning maneuver is underway
and you don't want to interfere with it or get hit by the boom
as it swings, often with tremendous force, over your head.

The decision to go up on deck is also a commitment to become
a contributing member of the crew in whatever it is doing at
the time. A crew of thirteen people sounds like a big crew with
plenty of backup help available. This is not true on a GL70. It
takes many hands to turn this boat. When the decision is made
to change sails, tack or jibe, it doesn't matter how tired you are
or what little or no sleep you've had. You suck it up and try your
hardest to put the boat in a position to win. You have a job to do
and all your shipmates are counting on you to do it correctly. A
well-executed maneuver is a source of pride to everyone onboard.
A manuever done poorly is frustrating and undermines morale.

At this point, EVOLUTION is crossing over to the
Michigan side of the lake. They have decided not to bring
their new asymmetric sail aboard because they don't feel there
will be wind conditions suited to its unique configuration.
EVOLUTION carries five symmetrical sails, as allowed by
class rules. As they sail along the Michigan shoreline during
the afternoon, they try to take advantage of any thermal
breezes which might be caused by the interaction of the cool
air over the water and the solar-heated Michigan shoreline.

The next big landmark, Point Betsie Light, is off our starboard
bow. We have definitely crossed over to the Michigan side of the
lake and now begin seeing many of the sights which make the
Chicago Mac so much fun. Point Betsie is actually very near the
city of Frankfort, MI and not far from a tremendous inland lake,
Crystal Lake. The next big destination will be the Manitou Islands
and the 45th parallel call-in point.

As has been the case for the last twenty four hours, we are
in the lead, with EVOLUTION in hot pursuit. It seems as
if NITEMARE, although further behind, is also becoming

a contender. Although we don't have any information on the rest of the fleet, I'm sure there are a number of duels in progress. One of the interesting facets of a yacht race is the competition which takes place between boats further back in the pack. Sometimes the most spirited race is not between the leaders, but among those crews trying to avoid being last.

As we pass Point Betsie, we can now make out the distinctive face of Sleeping Bear Sand Dunes. From the water and five miles offshore, you can appreciate how large it really is. The entire face of this large peninsula is covered completely with sand. It appears to slant at about a forty-five degree angle as it descends from the ridge to the water's edge. Truly beautiful!

Jack's recollection of Sunday:

"At this point in the race, it was fairly easy going. We were sailing downwind in moderate pressure. The course starts to condense a bit and it is light out. This is where you get to see how you have sailed through the night and if anyone has made a gain or loss. We maintained our lead on the fleet and were now just working at staying between our nearest competitors and the next waypoint (Point Betsie) on the course. Mentally, it is tough to be in the lead when the other boats are still within striking distance. You have to be good at delegating to the rest of the crew. The crew also have to be skilled enough to do their jobs at a high level or else the boat slows down. We have a group of talented guys who can do multiple tasks onboard. So this means we can continue to sail at a high level through watch changes.

Rest periods for the crew at this point of the race were also important. Human ballast on the rail was no longer a huge concern. So to have four people below resting was not hurting righting moment or boat speed. Plus, our forecast was predicting a long race and a long night ahead of us. Crew rest was key during the day on Sunday. One of the things that we did well during the race was stick to and execute our pre-race strategy. An area we could have improved upon was our downwind sail selection. We were working with our 1.5 A-sail and trying to figure out when it was effective or not as effective as compared with the symmetrical spinnakers. This process was strictly a trial and error process throughout the race. In hindsight, it is easy to see that we utilized the A-sail too much and should have switched to the #2S anytime we were sailing at 140 to 145 degrees true wind angle."

MEET THE BOAT & CREW
CHANCE USA 97503

Another one of the owners of a GL70 is Mike Brotz (Bio, page 152) out of Sheboygan, WI. He races his boat in both Mackinac races each year. It is a family affair with him, his son and daughter.

Chance.

CHANCE Crew List-2007 Chicago to Mackinac Race

James Zimmer......................... Sheboygan, WI
Jack Murphy .... Woodstock, ILL
Mike Brotz .... Kohler, WI
Adam Brotz............................. Bayside, WI
Garrett Forkner...................... Waterford, WI
Hans Graff.............................. Sheboygan, WI
Doug Steffenson..................... Wilmette, IL
Jim Allen .... Chicago, Ill
Susie Fieweger .... Fox Point, WI
Tom McGrath......................... Chicago, ILL
Olof Andersson .... Chicago, IL
Bob Bailey.............................. Lake Angelus, MI
Michael Considine................. Chicago, IL

J.B. Schumaker is a **PIED PIPER** crew member who has worked with Ben throughout the spring and summer preparing the boat for the upcoming races. In addition to being a highly skilled sailor, he is also a lot of fun. He started sailing when he was very young. His father has won many Mackinac races, as well as some one-design racing locally. He is the one who got J.B. into the sport and sent him to New York for his first big regatta, the Optimist Nationals when he was nine years old, placing seventh. There were 60 boats on the starting line for that event.

J.B.'s feelings about racing on **PIED PIPER**, in his own words:

"Sailing on **PIED PIPER** has been a great experience for me. I had the privilege of taking care of the boat in Muskegon where it was out of the water, working to get it prepared for the season. I have worked in many parts of the sailing industry from coaching to working at a sail loft. But, by far, the best experience I have had thus far is working on this boat. Sailing on a boat with this much history gives you that extra motivation to make each event as professional as possible. When you work on a boat every day, you

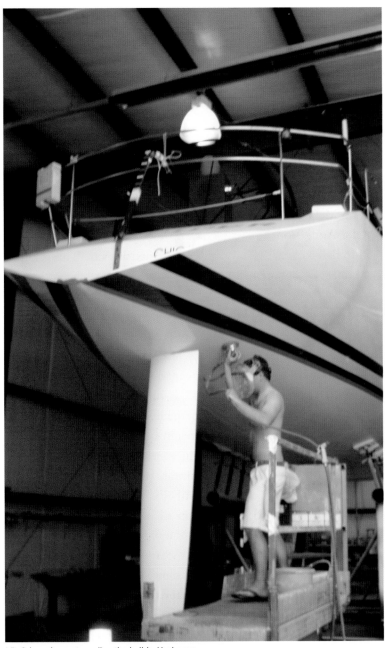

J.B. Schumaker wet sanding the hull in Muskegon.

Andy McCormick at the helm

know it inside and out. So when it gets to race day, you have that much more pride. I really enjoy racing on the boat because we are all friends and many of the crew are from Bayview Yacht Club where I grew up. The attitude on both boats named **PIED PIPER**, the Melges 24 and the GL70, is always to get better whether we win or not. This is an attitude that I feel is the best attribute for the team."

One of the most significant innovations aboard today's boats is a Global Positioning System (GPS). Of course, a GPS is of great value to the cruising sailor who is often out of sight of land and in unfamiliar waters.

Andy McCormick (Bio, page 143) is our navigator. As mentioned previously, he is an Old Goat and equally important, he personally oversaw the construction of the boat in California. No one is more familiar with this boat and this race course than Andy. As pictured, he also doubles as a helmsman during the race. He keeps us on the rhumb line while constantly re-plotting our course to the next waypoint and checking weather all along the route. The GPS system onboard is one of the various tools at his disposal located in the navigation station on the aft starboard side of the main cabin.

The computer screen of the GPS shows the exact position of the boat and any surrounding land masses. The ability to zoom in and out also helps identify the precise location of the boat in relation to its ultimate destination. The zoom-in feature enables the sailor to determine the water depth ahead. Although

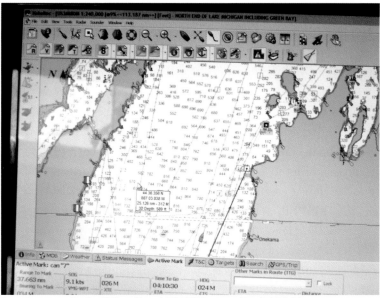

Computer screen showing GPS position of PIED PIPER approaching Point Betsie

all boats also use a separate depth sounder with a reading
instrument in a through-hull fitting to determine the depth
immediately under the boat, the GPS will reveal water depth
all around the present position as copied from data previously
believed reliable. Because water depths vary from year-to-year,
however, surrounding depths as indicated on the GPS screen
should only be used as a general reference and not considered
necessarily precisely accurate down to the foot measure.

For racers, the GPS has been revolutionary because it levels
the competition between boats. Prior to the advent of GPS, in
long distance races particularly, the ability of the navigator
onboard was a genuine differentiator. Today, all competitors
use similar GPS instruments and obtain similar and very
accurate information. The other benefit is the ability to
draw a rhumb line using GPS. A rhumb line is a straight line
extending from a boat's position to another position called

the "waypoint." The waypoint may be the eventual destination or an interim point on the way to the ultimate destination.

In the graphic on page 65, PIED PIPER is shown as a green boat in the lower right part of the GPS screen. It is on the rhumb line which, in this case, extends to a waypoint south of South Manitou Island. This is very important in distance racing because a slight difference in heading from the bearing of the rhumb line and the boat, can necessitate that the boat make a correction in its heading in order to arrive at the waypoint. Such a correction takes time traveling a greater distance than absolutely necessary. As you see, PIED PIPER, at this time, was precisely on the rhumb line.

After passing Point Betsie, our sights are on one of the most difficult segments of the race, the Manitou Passage. This is a traditional shortcut route taken between the northern part of Lake Michigan and Grays Reef. It lies between the western shore of the State of Michigan and two offshore islands, North Manitou Island and South Manitou Island. This portion is tricky because of the unpredictable wind patterns caused by these two large islands on the western side of the passage. Many times, Mackinac racers have been becalmed in this stretch, allowing those behind to catch up or, even worse, pass them. As we approach the southern opening to the passage, we are concerned that our lead will be endangered by light air conditions ahead. As we begin tacking into the passage, we can see that EVOLUTION is definitely beginning to close the gap on us.

As is the case every year, there is much discussion aboard EVOLUTION as to whether she should sail inside or outside the Manitou Passage. Terry Kohler, the boat's owner, is usually the person to bring the topic before the crew. This year is no exception. Although EVOLUTION only sailed outside the passage once before, with poor results, it is always an option that should be considered. The participants in this discussion are Terry Kohler, Peter Reichelsdorfer, Dan Reichelsdorfer, the three watch captains.

GL 70								
Sail number	Boat Name	Yacht Type	Length	Club	ORR	45th Call-in Time	Corrected Time	
USA 41104	Pied Piper	Great Lakes 70	68	Lake Geneva Yacht Club	1.164	Sunday - 19:14	33:38:22	1
USA 70	Evolution	Great Lakes 70	68	Sheboygan Yacht Club	1.168	Sunday - 19:14	33:45:18	2
USA 52701	Windancer	Great Lakes 70	68	Muskegon Yacht Club	1.166	Sunday - 19:37	34:08:39	3
USA 18970	Nitemare	Great Lakes 70	68	Chicago Yacht Club	1.147	Sunday - 20:10	34:13:07	4
USA 25168	Stripes	Santa Cruz 70	66.85	Bayview Yacht Club	1.151	Sunday - 20:10	34:20:17	5
USA 50045	Blow 'em to Smithereens	Great Lakes 70	68	Burnham Park Yacht Club	1.156	Sunday - 20:14	34:33:51	6
USA 28115	Mirage	Great Lakes 70	68	Chicago Yacht Club	1.157	Sunday - 20:27	34:50:41	7
USA 97503	Chance	Great Lakes 70	68	Sheboygan Yacht Club	1.152	Sunday - 20:42	34:58:56	8
USA 77984	Pororoca	Great Lakes 70	68	Chicago Yacht Club	1.121	Sunday - 22:19	35:51:11	9
USA 87666	Thirsty Tiger	Great Lakes 70	68	Chicago Yacht Club	1.153	Sunday - 22:22	36:56:03	10
Number of boats registered in this section: 10								

This chart, taken from the official Chicago Yacht Club Mackinac Race website, shows the order and times of the calls made at the 45th parallel in the 2007 GL70 race.

The decision becomes clear. Because the breeze continues from the southwest, they will go through the passage rather than around it again this year.

Shortly thereafter, NITEMARE and others enter the passage with much fighting between boats for position in a faint breeze. NITEMARE gets stalled over and over again. On one occasion, STRIPES comes within one boat length. NITEMARE jibes to starboard, catches a puff and moves five miles ahead of STRIPES. As John Stanley aboard NITEMARE says, "That's the way these boats are. Get a little breeze and they can take off."

This body of water is also significant because the racing boats reach the 45th parallel while in the passage. The 45th parallel is the exact point on the earth's surface marking the half way point between the Equator and the North Pole. Distance races usually specify a call-in point where the boats report into race headquarters with their VHF radios after they have reached an agreed upon destination. It is often the rounding of a weather buoy, a lighthouse, an island, or a temporarily installed floating marker.

In the Chicago to Mackinac Race, the 45th parallel, located with GPS, is the designated call-in point. A call-in point provides helpful information to those administering the race from shore (the race committee.) The call-in allows the race committee to know the location of the first boat at a specific time which can alert them to know if the fleet appears to be early or late compared to previous years. It also helps the committee account for each boat as it calls in. Of course there are bragging rights for the first boat that calls in ahead of the other boats in her class.

The following excerpt appeared on July 16, 2007 on the *Chicago Sun Times* website:

> *WINDQUEST ran well ahead of the bulk of the fleet in the annual race from Chicago to Mackinac Island, Mich. Only Equation, also in Section 1, had made the 45th call-in by the time WINDQUEST finished. Shortly after, EVOLUTION and PIED PIPER, made their 45th call-in. They and the rest of the Great Lakes 70s were expected to finish overnight.*

On the 45th Parallel Chart, you'll notice that WINDANCER called in exactly thirty minutes after PIED PIPER. This came as a shock to me because we did not see WINDANCER behind us as we advanced northward in the passage. The crew aboard WINDANCER had made a very gutsy and risky decision to sail west of the Manitous and take the longer route to avoid the lighter air in the passage. They made this decision in the hope that there would be stronger air in open water.

The following is a description of the action by Sam Nedeau aboard WINDANCER:

"After a number of stops and starts on Sunday, we find ourselves going into the Manitou Passage with several GL70s in sight, ahead of us. We also have THIRSTY TIGER, POROROCA and STRIPES behind us. At this point of the race, we are downwind tacking (gibing) and sailing our polar angles. Every year it is prudent to discuss sailing outside the Manitou Islands. It is a shorter distance to sail up the passage, but in certain conditions, it can pay to leave the Tous (Manitous) to starboard and go outside for more breeze. To do this, it is necessary to calculate the decision miles and miles beforehand to be properly set up for it. About 30 miles prior to South Manitou Bell Buoy, we start our contemplation and calculation.

It is a big gamble, but we are so far behind NITEMARE, MIRAGE and EVOLUTION that it is a calculated risk we have to consider. The funny thing about sailing with family is that arguments often arise. With two older brothers, a father, and three nephews aboard, this race is no exception. While our arguments are not overly violent, we are fortunate that we are all mature adults, though we do not always act like it. The decision to go outside the Manitou Passage is agreed upon by all the Nedeau family aboard. The icing on the cake is when WINDANCER's navigator, Jay VanderWall, calculates that, based upon the angles we are sailing, it is possible that going outside will actually be a bit shorter in distance.

Off we sail on port tack, in a dying breeze and a setting sun. By doing this, we actually cross the 45th parallel before several of our class members and, therefore, call in before they do. This leaves a lot of misrepresentation as to who is leading and who is behind. We are behind, no doubt about it. WINDANCER is now just well west of the rest of the class.

I had only gone once previously outside the Manitous in a Mac race. In 1985 we did it aboard INTREPID with mixed results. In 1996, we watched Dick Jennings on PIED PIPER do it successfully while moving from last to first place. We sailed, at sunset, into the passage and into a huge race boat parking lot that year.

WINDANCER keeps moving all night and, even though the wind is not strong, we never fall below three knots boat speed and a few times have her up to six or seven knots. Coming from the West to get back into the Tous is a little tricky and, with the water levels low, we are pretty conservative. As we reach eastward, we start running into more and more flat spots, which indicate that maybe it is light air inside the passage. Sure enough, when the sun rises, WINDANCER finds herself among the leaders near the same East-West line.

PIED PIPER, EVOLUTION, NITEMARE and MIRAGE are miles off to the East, but not too far to the North. BLOW 'EM TO SMITHEREENS, STRIPES, CHANCE, POROROCA and THIRSTY TIGER are all within a mile of us from North to South, with BLOW 'EM TO SMITHEREENS and STRIPES within shouting distance. The gamble has paid off, kind of. It appears as though the front boats sat without wind and the rear boats have caught up. The leaders must have reached with the light south breeze to the east while the other boats sailed up from behind. The kicker is that we are all becalmed.

Now, the question is, from which direction will the wind fill in? If the wind fills in from the East, PIED PIPER, EVOLUTION, NITEMARE and MIRAGE will look very good. If the wind fills in from the West, WINDANCER, BLOW 'EM TO SMITHEREENS and STRIPES will benefit. To our dismay the wind fills in from the East. The race is over for WINDANCER.

We had a nice sail and many would've/could've discussions. Luck is always involved in Mackinac racing, but skill is too. My father has a limited number of Mackinac races left in him and therefore, this year's Chicago to Mac crew was more Nedeau family oriented. We put ourselves in a position to do very, very well had the wind filled in from the West. We really cannot complain. I will always remember going outside the Tous. We heard loons and later some wolves howling on South Fox Island."

MEET THE BOAT & CREW
WINDANCER USA 52701

60th Anniversary WINDANCER Crew-2007 Chicago to
Mackinac Race

Carl Peterson .... Spring Lake, MI

Jay VanderWall .... Midland , MI

John Nedeau Sr. .... North Muskegon, MI

Matt Smith............................... West Bloomfield, MI

Thomas Bebee .... Spring Lake, MI

Tyler Nedeau .... Lake Bluff, IL

John Bousfield .... Spring Lake, MI

Jim Key .... Coopersville MI

Samuel (Sam) Nedeau .... Evanston, IL

John Nedeau Jr. .... Lake Bluff, IL

Nicholas (Nick) Nedeau .... Lake Bluff, IL

Matt Bombery .... Ann Arbor, MI

John Nedeau III .... Lake Bluff, IL

Drew Shea .... Wilmette, IL

WINDANCER.

One of the more significant dramas being played out during this race is the fact that this is the 60th anniversary Chicago to Mackinac Race for WINDANCER's skipper, 76-year-old, John Nedeau (Bio, page 167). One cannot imagine the experiences John has encountered on Lake Michigan while being "out there" in every conceivable circumstance since 1947. John is a modest man and it is difficult to pry any information out of him when asked to talk about himself. The following is a short interview I had with him aboard WINDANCER after the race:

Q. John, how were you able to complete 60 CHI Mac Races?

A. It all starts with a good wife.

Q. What's it like being out there all those years on these boats?

A. The fact is I just feel blessed. To be able to do something 60 years in a row, it let's you realize how close to God you should be. All the rest is cosmetics. I feel so blessed and so lucky. I can't describe it.

Q. What's it like to have family involved with your sailing?

A. I've always had family with me. This is just part of what we do. When I bought our first big boat, one night at dinner, I asked what we would name the boat? My daughter, Mindy, came up with the name WINDANCER. That's what it's been. All family.

Q. Can you separate your love of sailing from your love of racing sailboats?

A. I don't like to go for a sail. I like to race. I still go down to the yacht club on Wednesday night and jump on a boat. I can usually get a ride.

Q. How long, aside from family members, have your crew members been with you?

A. Some of my crew have been with me over 30 years. Jay VanderWall started in 1978. We had a knock down shortly after the start of the Bayview Mackinac Race one year and the radio direction finder broke. Jay, as a young man on the boat, figured out a way to fix it. There are many examples through the years of great teamwork by everyone.

Q. What is it like to compete in the GL70 Class?

A. I really like the guys in the GL70 fleet. I go to an owner meeting and say, "John, you know everyone here is smarter than you are." It is an incredible group of people. They settle differences amicably. When I bought WINDANCER (VII) from Terry Kohler, I sent a check for it sight unseen before the lawyers wrote up the papers. I knew the integrity of the people involved. I have tremendous respect for them and its fun to compete against them.

JULY 15, 2007-7:37 PM
NORTH MANITOU SHOAL LIGHT
LATITUDE 45 00.812N, LONGITUDE – 085 57.620W
COG: 32 DEGREES, SOG: 7.7 KNOTS

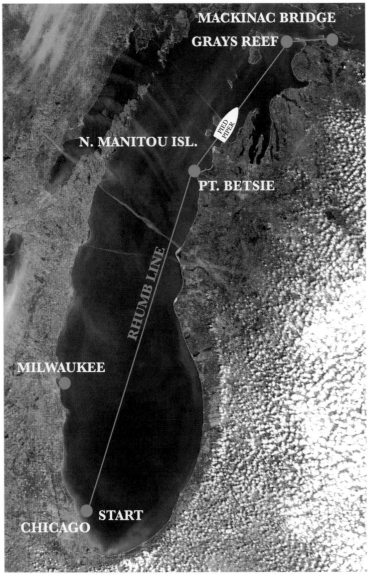

Photo courtesy of Liam Gumley, Space Science and Engineering Center, University of Wisconsin-Madison.

North Manitou Shoal Light.

Sunset in the Manitou Passage.

Now, the battle is joined between **PIED PIPER** and **EVOLUTION**. Until now, although these two boats have had a singular focus on one another, they have been many miles apart. Not anymore. We are both in the passage jibing back and forth alongside South Manitou Island in slightly different but very light breezes. We want to keep **EVOLUTION** behind us and escape the doldrums in the passage as soon as possible. The escape will be confirmed when we pass the North Manitou Shoal Light shown in the photo on page 75. The tension has increased significantly among the crew because of the proximity of our closest competitor. I couldn't, however, avoid being somewhat distracted by the sight of this lighthouse. It is the most unique I have ever seen.

While sailing in the passage, **EVOLUTION** sees **PIED PIPER** ahead. She appears to be in a hole (no wind) north of the North Manitou Shoal Light. Later, **EVOLUTION** begins to move closer, but eventually loses sight of her competitor in the darkness.

MEET THE BOAT & CREW
POROROCA USA 77984

The only non-Santa Cruz 70 in the fleet, POROROCA, a Nelson Marek 68, is skippered by 79 year old Gene McCarthy (Bio, page 162) and his partner, Bob Zeman (Bio, page 163). Both Gene and Bob are highly experienced and accomplished sailors.

POROROCA.

After a short time, the EVOLUTION crew decides to tack away, hoping to find some breeze not available to us or them while they remained directly on our stern. We can tell they have tacked to starboard because the only lights visible are her masthead, stern and green bow light. Their tactic doesn't seem to help because, despite the feeling that we are hardly moving at all, we notice that

Walter Wesley
Glenn McCarthy
Marco Lucchinetti
Bob Zerman
Jarrett Aitmin
David Smith
Neal Turluck
Doug McKirahan
Amy Hogue
Jack Rickard
Bill Kellner
Ted Weitzel
Gail Turluck
Gene McCarthy

The crew of POROROCA.

her running lights are becoming smaller. Later, they tack back onto port turning her green bow light to red.

Jack decides during this period to change our headsail to our lightest spinnaker. Although, the foredeck crew usually have a flashlight to shine on the headsail so the helmsman can see how it is flying, Jack asks them not to shine the light so as not to alert the EVOLUTION crew of our recent sail change which

is working very well for us. It is a good decision. We definitely accelerate away from them until their lights completely disappear from sight. We are jubilant that we have, while facing the most serious threat to our lead during the whole race, escaped into the darkness while maintaining our lead.

Eric Vigrass at the helm

78

The jubilation hasn't lasted long because we are becalmed once again. It is around midnight and Eric Vigrass (Bio, page 146), a native of Port Huron, Michigan is on the foredeck attempting to get some air into the headsail. After a fruitless and prolonged effort, he goes off watch. While walking past those of us on deck he says, "Good luck f-ckers." It breaks the somber mood and we all get a good laugh.

MEET THE BOAT & CREW
EVOLUTION USA 70

This is a photo of EVOLUTION taken by Matt Smith while racing aboard WINDANCER.

EVOLUTION Crew List

Jason Deiner	Sheboygan, WI
Peter Reichelsdorfer	Sheboygan, WI
Dan Reichelsdorfer	Sheboygan, WI
Greta Schanen	Port Washington, WI
Steve Orlebeke	Pewaukee, WI
Richard Reichelsdorfer	S. Belgium, WI

Greg Hartlmeier .... Whitefish Bay, WI
Eugene Altweis........................ Burlington, WI
Mark Wessel........................... Sheboygan, WI
Tony Orlebeke .... Sheboygan, WI
Terry Kohler .... Sheboygan, WI
Jason Bemis............................ Sheboygan, WI
Mark Wiss .... Middleton, RI
Michou Reichelsdorfer .... Sheboygan , WI

Jack recalls sailing through the Manitou Passage

"We started heading through the Manitous at dusk. We were hopeful that if we still had the lead out of the Manitous, we might be able to extend our lead to the finish. It was not to be the case as just the opposite happened. The wind died all around us bringing our competitors closer to us as darkness fell. This was the start of a very long night of limited or no wind."

Provisioning

Bob Wiesen offers tips on provisioning a racing boat for both buoy and distance races. Here is his advice in his own words:

Bob Wiesen with chart.

"Sea condition, wind velocity and direction, race distance, galley equipment, food & beverage weight allowance and waste control must be considered prior to heading for the harbor to race. Bob has been the provisioner and chef on PIED PIPER from the start. Keeping the crew properly hydrated and fed are vital to winning any race.

Preparation for a series of day buoy races is totally different than for a distance race up to six days, or overnight races, whether on the Great Lakes, in the Caribbean, Mexico or the Mediterranean. An over-six day race requires a different agenda and menu altogether and is not taken into consideration here. Day races simply require a hardy white meat sandwich with chips for a between race lunch, fruit and cheese in the afternoon, and electrolytes, meaning water, lots of water. Bob and Jack Jennings carefully observe crewmembers after leaving the dock for the duration of any race. If a person is dehydrated, he will not perform to his maximum capacity. Bob pushes water in front of the crew constantly.

On distance races, under seven days, or overnight races anywhere in the world, Bob states that careful menu preparation is required of the provisioner after analyzing expected weather and sea conditions. With warm days and nights, a lighter fare with fruit and water, is important in order to keep crew energy levels high and minds alert, particularly during night hours. Since most sailors do not take salt tablets on hot days, a good substitute are chips and pretzel rods with heavy sodium content. Cold days and nights require the provisioner to serve meals and snacks with more carbohydrates, higher fiber, higher calorie levels and more natural sugar from a variety of fruits.

In both warm and cold weather conditions, crew member sleep is a factor in winning races. Good sailors stay on deck for the duration of a day race. In distance races, however, going off watch for a couple of hours of sleep below deck is important. Rarely during a sailor's off watch, is he not called on deck for a sail change or tacking/gibing maneuvers. When the crew comes on deck, being awake and alert is critical for safety and performance reasons. What the sailor has consumed will determine if he is at his peak physical and mental level to win the race. Bob maintains that white meat, hearty bread, chips, pretzel rods, fruit, granola bars for an occasional energy hit and water are important components when provisioning a winning racing yacht.

Bob, Dick Jennings, Andy McCormack and Paul Snow, each PIED PIPER veterans, are members of the Island Goats Sailing Society of Chicago, and the Society of Mackinac Island Goats of Detroit. To become a member of either society, a sailor must have raced in at least 25 MAC races respectively. Members of both societies are commonly known and affectionately called "Double Goats." As of September, 2007 only 11 people in history are Double Goats, including the four sailors mentioned above.

MEET THE BOAT & CREW
THIRSTY TIGER USA 87666

Bert D'Ottavio (Bio, page 166) is the owner of the GL70, THIRSTY TIGER. Like NITEMARE, she is highly visible with her bright, shiny red hull. Bert prides himself on upgrading his boat with some major changes to the layout which he performed himself. In addition to being a highly successful yacht racer, he is also quite a craftsman.

THIRSTY TIGER & Chicago skyline.

Albert D'Ottavio .... Joliet, IL

Dave Henderson .... Sheridan, IL

Bob Warnecke .... Palatine, IL

Tony Diar Bakerli .... Chicago, IL

Ed Marshall .... Wheaton, IL

Rich Pecard .... Chicago, IL

Leo Pickar .... Chicago, IL

Eric Thoren .... Chicago IL

Jeff Dalsin .... Chicago, IL

Darius Barkauskas .... Downers Grove, IL

Luiz Kahl .... Grosse Point Woods, MI.

Ryan Gardner .... Kalamazoo, MI.

Robert Nutter .... Westchester, IL.

JULY 16th - 9:30 AM
GRAYS REEF LIGHT HOUSE
LATITUDE – 45 44.539N, LONGITUDE – 085 09.112W
COG: 7 DEGREES, SOG: 8.7 KNOTS

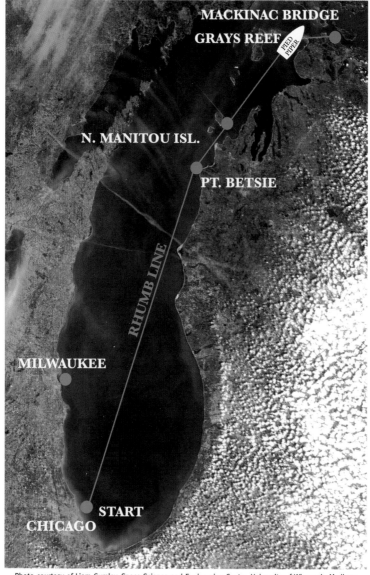

Photo courtesy of Liam Gumley, Space Science and Engineering Center, University of Wisconsin-Madison.

Gray's Reef Lighthouse.

Early Monday morning actually changes the entire outcome of the race. It is during the hours 1:00 a.m. to 4:00 a.m. Distance sailors always refer to these hours as money time. You and all your competitors are very tired and on the brink of exhaustion. You have finished two days and one night in open water while pushing the boat and yourself as hard as you can. The question becomes, "Who wants it the most?" On this night, with very little wind and fog creeping in, it seems that neither we nor our competitors will gain much distance on one another. So, although we are not moving much at all, it appears logical that EVOLUTION isn't moving either.

MEET THE BOAT & CREW
MIRAGE USA 28115

MIRAGE, owned by Rick Woodworth (Bio, page 158), Bill Dooley (Bio, page 159) and Eric Joost (Bio, page 160), is another one of the very competitive boats. Rick and Bill bought MIRAGE in 2002 and Eric became an owner in 2004. It has been a terrific experience. Rick thinks there is something about the GL70 boat design which makes for great competition. In certain conditions, they are faster than the wind speed itself. It's also a very easy platform for 15 people. These boats look good and there is a lot of balance in the class

Mirage.

MIRAGE Crew List-2007 Chicago to Mackinac race
Rick Woodworth...................... Northbrook, IL
Bill Dooley .... Glencoe, IL
Eric Joost................................ Chicago, IL
Jim Armstrong .... Lake Forest, IL

Dan Woodworth .... Chicago, IL
Mike Woodworth .... Glenview, IL
Matt Woodworth .... Glenview, IL
Tyler Woodworth .... Naperville, IL
Steven Sickler.......................... Chicago, IL
Brian Giegerich.......................Joliet, IL
Jon Flusser.............................. Lake Forest, IL
Mike Davis.............................. Chicago, Ill.
Tom Keegan .... Chicago, Ill

By this time, I have been on deck with no sleep for thirty five hours. I am on the port rail near the mast at about 1:00 a.m. when Mike Hoey says, "OK, iron man, you've made your point. Now, go below and get some sleep." It sounds like a really good idea, so down I go into the cabin where guys are asleep everywhere in bunks and on sail bags. The only bunks available are uppers. They have all been cranked up so that their occupants will not fall onto the cabin floor should the boat tack in heavy air. As I look at the small space between the upper bunk and the cabin roof, I can't imagine how I am going to get my 6'3" frame, clothed with three layers plus foul weather gear and boots, into that bunk. Dave Shriner sees my situation and says, "Step up onto the corner of J.B.'s bunk, but don't step on J.B." Getting enough height with that maneuver, I spring into the bunk and does it feel good! Jack is very generous this race and has provided pillows for each bunk, which, I learned is a luxury not usually permitted on **PIED PIPER**.

I am asleep in seconds until, after three hours, I am awakened for the next watch change at 4:00 a.m. It is Monday morning, the final day of the race. When I get topside, it is as black as ever and extremely foggy. I sit down on the starboard rail next to Brian Brophy, one of the original crewmen on **PIED PIPER**. As we sit there, having come from a relatively warm cabin, it seems very cold and everything is soaking wet. Water keeps pouring down on us from above. Brian looks at me and knows I think it is raining. Before I can comment, he says, "It's not rain. The water pouring down on us is heavy dew created by the fog and running down the mainsail onto our heads."

We are making slow headway in the dark and fog. Jack has returned to the deck and is at the wheel. Because I have been on deck most of the night, I am very tired and cold. It doesn't seem to matter how many layers of clothing you wear in the upper part of the Great Lakes at night. Even though the races are held in the middle of July, the dampness and cold air are quite a combination. It is something to be endured until sunrise.

For the first time in the race, I don't feel well. It seems the only alternative is to begin getting sugar into my system. I go below where Bob has a shelf filled with all kinds of snacks. I grab three of them and eat quickly. In about a half hour, the infusion of carbohydrates begins to work its magic and I feel good again. Luckily, after this brief episode, I have no other repercussions.

At about 4:30 a.m., as we sit silently on deck, Jack suddenly announces, "Boys. We're f-cked. EVO (EVOLUTION) has moved ahead of us." The news is devastating and instantly demoralizing. I just can't believe it. The last time we saw the other boat, before the fog filled in, we had gone so far ahead that they were out of sight. Now, in the darkness, as the fog is just beginning to burn off with the first, slight glimpse of a new day, there is EVOLUTION far off to our right and definitely further north.

Jack recalls EVOLUTION passing us:

"I remember we were doing our best to stay between our competition and the mark. With little or no wind, however, our ability to get into position was limited and the boats behind could have gained leverage to the right or left of us. This is what happened. The boats behind us gained leverage to the shore and, when day broke, they were able to sail in more wind at a higher speed and make a pass."

I immediately thought about some of the people I knew aboard EVOLUTION. Terry Kohler and Peter Reichelsdorfer were thirty to forty year veterans of this race. What did they do in the last three hours that we didn't do? Did they get a break over in their position to the right or did they create their own break through hard work and good decision making? Everyone was angry and upset.

Brian Brophy working the grinder

Even with little breeze, the crew on EVOLUTION has sailed the boat hard all night. Due to the heavy fog, they do not know where they are in relation to any other boats. As the fog begins to burn off with the first rays of sunlight on Monday morning, they can see they have passed PIED PIPER, which is off to their left and closer to Beaver Island. They also can see that NITEMARE has made substantial progress during the long night and is now behind them.

Shortly after the bad news about EVOLUTION, we also see that NITEMARE is making a move on us from the rear. There, in the growing sunlight is NITEMARE off to our right, but still behind us. She is actually between EVOLUTION and us. NITEMARE looks very foreboding with her bright and shiny red hull and huge, solid black spinnaker flying. Our lead, which we have held since the starting gun off Navy Pier, is lost and our new position, as the second place boat, is also instantly in jeopardy.

As always, EVOLUTION picks a destination for the next leg of the race, which, at this time, is Grays Reef. They want to maximize their Velocity Made Good (VMG) which is a racing term meaning, "The speed of a yacht relative to the waypoint it wants to reach, or toward or away from the wind." They know PIED PIPER is faster in heavy air, but also know EVOLUTION, at least in previous years, has had the advantage in existing light air conditions. As he looks over at PIED PIPER, Steve Orlebeke, one of EVOLUTION's crewmembers remarks, "If they get a shift, they'll win. If we get a shift, it'll be us." So, the outcome of the race, as both boats speed toward Grays Reef, is still in doubt.

While all this is happening, the sun is beginning its rapid ascent out of the lake directly ahead of us. How incredibly beautiful it is! With the sun's rising, the battle of warm rays against the cold and foggy surface of the water, is renewed for another day. This combination works magic in the eyes of a sailor in open water. As the air above the water's surface begins to warm, an airflow is created causing ripples on the previously smooth surface. Those ripples are heading straight for PIED PIPER and neither of our competitors. At our westerly position, we get the growing breeze first and off we go. Neither EVOLUTION nor NITEMARE are moving. Desperation immediately turns to joy. We are ecstatic as we resume the lead position once again.

MEET THE BOAT & CREW
NITEMARE USA 18970

Tom Neill (Bio, page 160) and his crew aboard NITEMARE have been extremely competitive year after year. Most of his key crew members have been sailing with him for many years. NITEMARE is the most sailed GL70 every summer season. In addition to the GL70 events, Tom and his guys race NITEMARE every Wednesday around the buoys throughout May to September. He attributes much of his success to the great amount of time he and his crew spend racing together.

NITEMARE.

Thomas Neill	Berkeley, IL
James Sugrue	Chicago, IL
Tim Corkell	Elmhurst, IL
John Stanley	Racine, WI
Kevin D'April	Northbrook, IL
Steve Diaz	Wheaton, IL

We've regained the lead and are sailing toward Grays Reef with Beaver Island on our left. It's amazing how large it is. It seems that we have sailed at nine knots alongside it for a long time. After about an hour, the wind shifts direction once again. The big beneficiary is EVOLUTION. The new wind is from such an angle that it permits EVOLUTION to make a cut diagonally across our bow, which lifts it toward the reef with much less distance to travel. It is just one of those fickle traits of nature which make yacht racing always interesting and always a difficult mental challenge.

Should we have anticipated a shift? Perhaps a frequent visitor to this particular body of water would have seen it in the past and known to anticipate it. Perhaps the veterans on EVOLUTION were counting on it, or perhaps it was unforeseen by all of us on PIED PIPER, and the crew of EVOLUTION as well. The bottom line is that this shift irrevocably put EVOLUTION in front of us to stay.

The conversation on PIED PIPER has now shifted to the topic of the handicap assigned to each boat prior to the race. One of our crew believes that EVOLUTION owes us 9.35 minutes. This means she will have to cross the finish line ahead of us by this amount of time or more to claim first place. Brian Brophy takes out his stop watch as we pursue EVOLUTION to the turning mark near the Grays Reef Light House. At that mark, they will head toward the Mackinac Bridge east of her position. In order to gauge how much of a lead she has on us, we will record the time when she gibes around the mark and compare that time to when we round. According to Brian, we round 8.5 minutes after her. If we can finish the race at anything under 9.35 minutes after them, we will win the race. At this point, we feel we can win.

As EVOLUTION rounds the buoy at Grays Reef, she races down in the puffs to maximize her speed to the next objective, the Mackinac Bridge. About seven miles from the bridge, she usually gets a lift and it is true in this race as well. As they glance back at PIED PIPER, which has also rounded at Grays Reef, it appears to them PIED PIPER is making up her time on them.

Jack's recollection at this point in the race:

"At this point we were following behind EVOLUTION. It was disappointing but our chances to win the race were still good because of the time allotment their boat owes ours due to their lighter weight and other factors measured by the ORR rule under which we were racing. Passing opportunities for the rest of the race would be limited because both boats were sailing in a constant breeze, in light of day and the course itself narrows your options for leverage. The conditions were very easy downwind in a moderate breeze."

JULY 16, 12:00 PM
THE RACE TO THE MACKINAC BRIDGE
LATITUDE 45 49.219N, LONGITUDE 084 43.205W
COG: 64 DEGREES, SOG: 8.9 KNOTS

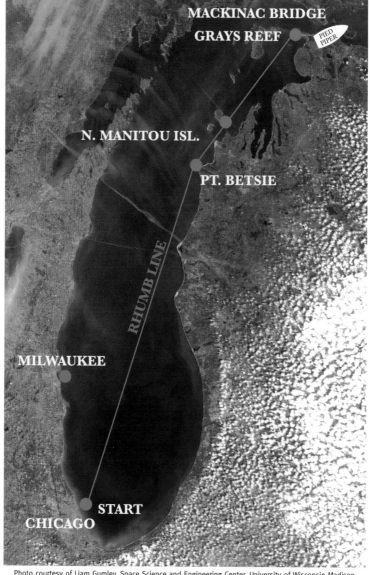

Photo courtesy of Liam Gumley, Space Science and Engineering Center, University of Wisconsin-Madison.

As we round the mark at Grays Reef, we have EVOLUTION clearly in our sights and NITEMARE off in the distance, seemingly far enough away so as not to interfere with the PIED PIPER/EVOLUTION duel. The crew on EVOLUTION is flying their full symmetrical spinnaker while we are using two headsails, our new asymmetrical sail and our staysail. The staysail is hoisted on its own halyard and the tack of the sail is attached to a fitting on the foredeck about five feet back from the headstay. The combination of these two sails, in certain conditions, and if properly trimmed, can help maximize boat speed.

We will not know if we have gained or fallen back on EVOLUTION until she passes under the Mackinac Bridge. We notice she is heading to the far right, which is actually the direction of the land mass across from Mackinac Island, Mackinaw City. Many times over the years, the passage under this huge bridge has been a precarious one for racers. Unexplainable dynamics between the wind and the superstructure of this enormous bridge have often caused lead boats to stall, sometimes for many hours. This unwelcome pause often allows competing boats in the rear to improve their positions and sometimes overtake the leader on their way to a last minute reversal of fortune. The question in our minds is, "Will EVOLUTION stall under the bridge this year?"

One of our guys in the back of the boat is shouting that NITEMARE is preparing to round Grays Reef behind us. According to the handicapping rules, we have to beat NITEMARE by forty minutes in order to preserve our position. So one of the guys watches her gibe around the mark and compares her rounding time with ours. According to his reading, NITEMARE rounded 36 minutes after us. The crewmembers aboard NITEMARE time it at 35 minutes as they watch PIED PIPER head for the southern shore before jibing for the bridge. They decide to maximize their speed by sailing low and staying in the breeze.

Eric Jochum on halyards

Now, we are caught in an emotionally traumatic situation. We have to finish less than 9:35 minutes behind EVOLUTION and more than 40 minutes ahead of NITEMARE. Although NITEMARE rounded thirty-six minutes after us, she still has many miles to the finish line. Hopefully she will be slowed along the remaining route by either a lessening of the wind or trim or gibing errors. We all know, however, there are very good sailors aboard both boats and human error on either boat is unlikely.

As I turn to look at EVOLUTION ahead of us, it occurs to me that our two boats have been within sight of each other for the entire forty-six hours of the race except for three hours last night during the fog. Most distance racers will tell you they often sail for many hours and sometimes even days without seeing other competing boats and here we are almost to the finish line and EVOLUTION and NITEMARE are still in plain sight.

Eric Jochum is one of the crew members I got to know quite well. His job is to tail the halyards. While Brian Brophy is pulling on the halyards in order to raise a sail, Eric takes up the slack and secures the line to a winch. Because his job is just aft of the mast and the normal spot for me is in the same location, we've spent a lot of time together. The younger brother of our bowman, Dave, he is also the youngest crewman aboard and a current member of the Fordham University sailing team.

It seems to me that EVOLUTION is going unnecessarily too far to the right before gibing back to go under the center span of the bridge. Jack thinks that we should follow their course exactly so we will travel the same distance and, hopefully, in similar wind speed. This is not the time to take another route

Photo of PIED PIPER under the Mackinac Bridge provided by Gretchen Dorian Photography

to the bridge in the hope that we will find better conditions
elsewhere. THIS IS the Mackinac Race! We have been racing
for 46 hours. The island is in plain view just beyond the bridge.
We can still win if we follow her course and sail faster.

We watch her gibe and head for the bridge. We have our stop
watches out once again. At the moment her mast is under the
center of the bridge, we begin counting how long it will take us
to reach the same spot. As always, when approaching the bridge,
EVOLUTION's objective is to cross under the bridge at a point
near the south main tower, thus avoiding any shallow water near
the South Graham Shoal, which is approximately one mile square
in size and lying north and east of the bridge.

Unlike previous years, she does not slow down, but maintains
her speed under the bridge and beyond. We keep sailing
the exact route of our predecessor toward Mackinaw City
and then gibe toward the bridge. When we are under the

center of the bridge, we realize EVOLUTION has picked up about a minute on us since the Grays Reef rounding.

Jack's Recollection under the Bridge:

At the bridge we knew the time allotment with EVOLUTION was going to be close. Sometimes the wind dies when you get to this point of the race, but not this year. The wind was actually on the increase. We sailed well at this point and executed a very successful gibe towards the finish line.

JULY 16, 12:30 PM
HARD LANDING IN THE HARBOR
LATITUDE 45 50.557N, LONGITUDE 084 37.714W
COG: 116 DEGREES, SOG: 9.2 KNOTS

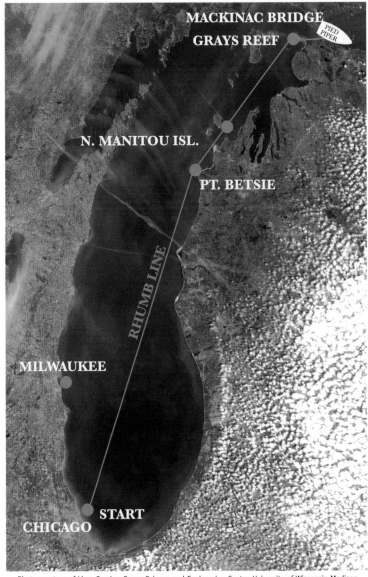

MACKINAC BRIDGE
PIED PIPER
GRAYS REEF

N. MANITOU ISL.

PT. BETSIE

RHUMB LINE

MILWAUKEE

START
CHICAGO

Photo courtesy of Liam Gumley, Space Science and Engineering Center, University of Wisconsin-Madison.

A restored lighthouse marking the southern end of the finish line.

As we gibe again, we are headed straight for the Grand Hotel, sitting majestically in its prominent position on the island. Its huge, white pillared porch is framed by the surrounding green foliage and blue sky above. I think to myself, what an incredible sight and vantage point from aboard a GL70 with her sails flying. Somebody yells out, "This is gonna be close." By this time, a number of our guys have their stopwatches out, waiting for EVOLUTION to execute her final gibe and make straight away for the finish line. Chicago Mackinac racers finish from the west side of the island. There is a small lighthouse on an islet across from the Iroquois Hotel. The Chicago Yacht Club's Race Committee sets up a tent next to the hotel and draws an imaginary line between its tent and the lighthouse opposite. When a finisher's bow crosses the line, a cannon is fired from shore, marking a completed voyage. We are waiting for the cannon's roar to set our watches. After we hear it, we know we have to cross in less than 9:35 minutes in order to win. We are now sailing away from the Grand Hotel and have one more gibe to make before finishing. Except for the guys steering and trimming the sails in the back of the boat, the rest of us are bunched up on the starboard rail and lying down so as to create the least amount of wind resistance. Jack is at the wheel with Mike Hoey and Perry Lewis at his side.

Brian begins calling out each minute that has elapsed since EVOLUTION's cannon salute. "One minute, two minutes, three minutes." We make our final gibe and are now heading straight for the finish line. It is extremely tense on the boat. After all the work, decision making and tactics employed, winning the Mackinac Race comes down to a very close victory or defeat. We can see the guys on EVOLUTION enter Mackinac Island's Outer Harbor, while lowering sails and motoring to her assigned boat slip. "Four minutes, five minutes, six minutes." We are moving well and, although hard to gauge the distance to the finish line, it seems we will finish under our time deadline.

I am lying on one of the sail covers on the bow ahead of the mast next to J.B. Schumaker. He is asking me what it has been like for me to sail with them on a GL70 for the first time. I reply that it has been an enormous thrill that surpassed all my wildest expectations. I tell him that it has been an incredible experience to be on such a large boat and part of a large crew. With the exception of the 2005 Bayview Mackinac Race aboard the J105, VENOM, I've always been a small boat sailor. He reminds me that all the guys on PIED PIPER started out sailing Lightnings and other small boats.

"Seven minutes, eight minutes."

We can see the people on the race committee to our left and one of them is ready to fire the cannon upon our crossing. "Nine minutes, five seconds, ten seconds." Mike Hoey runs up and pushes the main sail completely to the port side of the boat, thus giving us maximum speed with the present wind angle. "Twenty seconds, twenty five seconds." Dave Jochum, our bow man and the furthest forward on the deck yells, "Fire the gun, we're over, fire the gun!" Just at that instant, a boat from Shepler's Ferry Service comes roaring out of the outer harbor on its way back to Mackinaw City on the mainland. Dave yells, "It's gonna block the committee's sight of our bow, fire the gun!" Just as he predicts, the ferry cuts between us and the race committee, temporarily blocking their sight down the finish line. By then, we have obviously passed it, but still hear no cannon. After the ferry passes and the race committee can see PIED PIPER once again, the cannon is finally fired. According to our calculations, we exceeded our deadline by twenty seconds. We are in second place.

Jack's Recollection of the finish:

"We finished the race going fast. We were the fourth boat out of 290 boats to arrive at Mackinac Island."

The disappointment felt by everyone on PIED PIPER is overwhelming. It seems we might have lost our first place position in the Mackinac Race partially because of a quirky set of circumstances unexpected and completely out of our control. As joyous as I am to complete the race, it seems like someone just ripped the heart right out of my chest. I wish there is something, anything I can do to reverse the outcome.

As Jack turns on the engine and we begin to lower the sails, it is a very quiet boat except for some swearing. Everyone has given their all for two days and nights and

Jack Jennings crossing the finish line.

really believed we would win this race until two minutes ago. What a blow! It is hard to grasp the bitter reality that the race is over for PIED PIPER. There's nothing more we can do.

As we're taking the sails down, Andy receives a call on the VHF radio that we are to be boarded immediately upon tying up at our boat slip for a boat inspection by the Race Committee's Safety Committee. Every organized yacht race has a list of rules governing an upcoming race called the "Sailing Instructions (SI)." All skippers must comply with these rules. Among the rules are also safety requirements. For a distance race of this length, the safety rules are quite extensive. J.B. and Ben swing into action by running down into the cabin to be sure everything is in order for the inspection. J.B. notices some belt life jackets are not in their proper place and calls for the others to be turned in immediately.

As we begin backing into our slip, I notice two young women standing next to it, each holding a clipboard. They are giggling and laughing and seem to be having the time of their lives. I surmise that they constitute the safety committee. Even before we have our dock lines secure, they attempt to come aboard, but are asked to wait until the boat is tied up properly. When they come aboard, they go straight into the cabin and are down there for about fifteen minutes. While they are still down there, Andy comes up to me and says they have found some violations and we will be penalized. I ask him what the violations are and he says he thinks it involves our safety flares. Shortly thereafter, they emerge from the cabin and exit the boat. We were to learn later that 18 boats received safety violations including the highly successful EQUATION and another GL 70, BLOW 'EM TO SMITHEREENS.

Jack is very solemn and quiet. The second place finish, followed within minutes by an unsatisfactory safety inspection, is a lot of bad news to process in such a short time. Although totally absorbed in the new, harsh realities, he looks over at me and says, "Tom, I hope this race was a good experience for you." To which I reply, "I had the time of my life and am very grateful for the opportunity." The protest hearing, regarding the safety committee's report, is to be held in a short time. Then, we will know how it will affect our finishing position.

Although the crew of EVOLUTION knows they have crossed the finish line in first place, they are very concerned about NITEMARE and her progress down the Straits of Mackinac. This is becoming an even greater concern because the wind is building. She has to give NITEMARE forty five minutes. While sitting on their boat in the harbor, they watch NITEMARE cross the finish line forty minutes later to claim the prize as the 2007 Chicago to Mackinac Race winner in the GL70 Class. Now, we have lost first and second place and are holding precariously onto third, pending the outcome of the protest hearing.

I climb up onto the dock and begin walking along the pier. Ahead of me by about ten feet is Dave Jochum heading in the same direction. He is talking to himself and waving his arms with angry gestures. It actually looks like he is in a street fight with an imaginary opponent. He is a very intense guy. He gives everything 120% effort and the outcome of this race has him talking to himself. I keep a safe distance behind him and watch this display as we walk along. It didn't let up. It was not a brief spurt of disappointment.

When I return to the boat, Jack has already left for the protest hearing. I am completely exhausted after a forty-seven hour race with three hours of sleep. Right then and there, I know I won't have the energy to either deliver the boat to Port Huron for next week's race from there back up to Mackinac Island nor will I participate in that race scheduled for the following Saturday. I decide to go over to the mainland and find some way back to the Detroit area and home. An hour later, while I am walking with my sea bag to take a ferry over to the mainland, Dave Jochum happens to be ahead of me again. The intensity and gesturing has not subsided.

Jack's Recollection of the Safety Committee Protest Hearing:

"The positive feeling you usually have after completing a Mackinac Race was not going to last very long this year. Shortly after the finish, we were notified that we were to be inspected by the Chicago Yacht Club Race Committee. At first, I was not too worried about this inspection because I knew our boat was well prepared and that safety was at the forefront of our preparation. Ben and J.B. had worked very hard preparing the boat and I felt confident we would pass the inspection. During the inspection, the inspector was rude and condescending to Ben (our boat captain). Her actions and the manner in which she treated him were a disgrace to her position. It left a very bitter taste in my mouth about returning to the Chicago Race next year."

After crossing from the island on the ferry, I rent a motel in Mackinaw City and schedule a flight out of Pellston Regional Airport for the following morning, which will depart at 6:30 a.m. It is now about 4:00 p.m. when I call Jack on his cell to tell him I will not be sailing in next week's race. He had told me previously he had actually overbooked the next race by one crewman, so my absence would be covered by a very able sailor. He says he

GL 70

Sail	Yacht	Americap	City, State	45th Call-in Time	Finish Time	Elapsed Time	Corrected	
USA 18970	Nitemare	1.147	Berkeley, Illinois	Sunday - 20:10	Monday - 13:10:34	46:50:34	53:43:43	1
USA 70	Evolution	1.168	Sheboygan, Wisconsin	Sunday - 19:14	Monday - 12:23:37	46:03:37	53:47:54	2
USA 77984	Pororoca	1.121	Chicago, Illinois	Sunday - 22:19	Monday - 14:45:03	48:25:03	54:16:33	3
USA 28115	Mirage	1.157	Northbrook, Illinois	Sunday - 20:27	Monday - 13:20:54	47:00:54	54:23:46	4
USA 25168	Stripes	1.151	Ann Arbor, Michigan	Sunday - 20:10	Monday - 13:51:27	47:31:27	54:42:01	5
USA 97503	Chance	1.152	Kohler, Wisconsin	Sunday - 20:42	Monday - 14:10:58	47:50:58	55:07:21	6
USA 50045	Blow 'Em to Smithereens	1.156	Niles , Illinois	Sunday - 20:14	Monday - 13:49:11	47:29:11	55:07:22 **	7
USA 87666	Thirsty Tiger	1.153	Joliet , Illinois	Sunday - 22:22	Monday - 14:11:38	47:51:38	55:10:59	8
USA 52701	Windancer	1.166	North Muskegon, Michigan	Sunday - 19:37	Monday - 14:02:56	47:42:56	55:38:10	9
USA 41104	Pied Piper	1.164	Niles , Illinois	Sunday - 19:14			DNF	10

PP Protest Pending	** Corrected time adjusted for penalties or redress

The chart is the order of finish from the 2007 Chicago to Mackinac Race website.

understands my reasons and that if I happen to change my mind during the coming week, am still welcome to come along. I ask him how the protest hearing came out and he replied, "They penalized us three positions which would drop us from third to sixth place. So, I told them PIED PIPER was withdrawing from the race."

I am shocked and find it hard to believe that our boat, which almost won the race four hours earlier, would be shown in the record books as "DNF," (Did Not Finish)! After returning to Detroit the next morning, I write the following farewell email to the crew:

To the crew of PIED PIPER,

Although Jack is prepared to have me join you for the Bayview Mackinac Race, I have requested that I be excused from participating as a crewman in this event. I will always be grateful for the many kindnesses extended to me by Jack, his father and all of you over the past couple of months. I have lived at Jack's house with you, practiced on four different days and been a fellow crewman for the 2007 Chicago to Mackinac race. I had the literal "time of my life" racing to Mackinac with you this past weekend. I am one of those fortunate few people who, thanks to you, had a dream come true. I raced with the best skipper and best crew and on the best boat I could ever imagine!

Your dedication, commitment and personal sacrifices gladly expended hour after hour in the pursuit of victory were overwhelming. I share your disappointment in the outcome and applaud Jack's decision to withdraw from the race in view of the decision taken by the race committee. I wish you every success on the upcoming race this weekend. I know you will have every chance of winning with a crew complete with highly skilled sailors.

I now turn to the task of recording my experiences and observations in a book that, hopefully, will live up to your high standards of excellence.

In regard to the race committee's treatment of PIED PIPER, I am reminded of one of my favorite speeches given by Theodore Roosevelt entitled, "The Man in the Arena":

> "It is not the critic who counts; not the man who points out how the strong man stumbles, or where the doer of deeds could have done them better. The credit belongs to the man who is actually in the arena, whose face is marred by dust and sweat and blood; who strives valiantly; who errs, who comes up short again and again, because there is no effort without error and shortcoming; but who does actually strive to do the deeds; who knows great enthusiasms, the great devotions; who spends himself in a worthy cause; who at the best knows in the end the triumph of high achievement, and who at the worst, if he fails, at least fails while daring greatly, so that his place shall never be with those cold and timid souls who neither know victory nor defeat."

Best of luck to you all,
Tom

OTHER GL70
RACING VENUES

QUEEN'S CUP
CHICAGO NOOD REGATTA
BAYVIEW MACKINAC RACE
BAY HARBOR REGATTA
CHICAGO VERVE CUP REGATTA

Great Lakes 70's racing together

Pictured above are some of the members of the Nedeau racing family. From left, Tyler Nedeau, Sam Nedeau, John Nedeau, John Nedeau, Jr. and John Nedeau III.

Although the official GL70 racing season begins with the Chicago NOOD in mid June, there is another race held in late June called, "The Queen's Cup Race." It is sponsored by the South Shore Yacht Club in Milwaukee and features a night race across Lake Michigan from Milwaukee, WI to Muskegon, MI. Many of the GL70s have participated in this race in the past. As mentioned earlier in this book, I was invited aboard WINDANCER, a GL70 from Muskegon to crew in two night races, the Tripp Memorial from Muskegon to Milwaukee on June 27 and the return two nights later in the 69th sailing of the Queen's Cup Race on June 29th.

It was very exciting for me for three reasons: I had never been aboard a GL70 in actual racing conditions. I had the opportunity to sail with John Nedeau and his many family members and the Tripp Memorial race was very fast thanks to a cold front which descended on Lake Michigan in the middle of the night providing 27 knot winds.

South Shore Yacht Club
2007 Queen's Cup Race
Class: All. PHRF (Time on distance)
Queens Cup: Division: Div 01
Start Time: Friday, June 29, 2007 18:50:00: Distance 66.6NM

Pos	Sail	Boat	Skipper	PH RF	Type	Finish	Elapsed	Corrected
1	50048	Main Street	Schanen,Bill	-21	J/145	09:28:29	14:38:29	15:01:48
2	52496	Sue	Moller,Jim	3	Farr 42	10:11:56	15:21:56	15:18:36
3	2615	Scout	Hummert,Jamie	15	Sydney	10:36:49	15:46:49	15:30:10
4	51115	TWISTER	Wake,Herb	-15	DuBois 50	10:03:42	15:13:42	15:30:21
5	48008	Wild Horses	Hennig,Rick	-30	1 D 48	09:54:11	15:04:11	15:37:29
6	52701	Windancer	Nedeau,John	-75	GL 70	09:13:24	14:23:24	15:46:39
7	77984	Pororoca	McCarthy,Gene	-54	N/M 68	10:10:55	15:20:55	16:20:51
8	28686	Windquest	DeVos,Doug	-156	MaxZ86	08:18:20	13:28:20	16:21:30
9	40888	Swiftsure	Ehlert,Ronald	0	N/M 50	11:46:55	16:56:55	16:56:55
TLE	52791	Promo	Kuber,John	-69	N/M 52			

Our crew of 16 aboard WINDANCER for the Queen's Cup Race the night of June, 29, 2007.

I was also permitted to bring one of my sailing buddies, Tom Grabowski, with me on the very fast Tripp Memorial Race. Another very prominent boat on the Great Lakes, the 86' WINDQUEST, was our primary competition and the one to watch. After an extremely slow start with very light air, the cold front hit at 11:30 p.m. and we were off for a great ride getting up to 15 knots boat speed in eight to ten foot waves. I stayed on deck all night and saw us descend on the harbor at Milwaukee just after sunrise with great speed. We edged out WINDQUEST on corrected time by eight seconds. Welcome to GL70 racing!

2007 QUEEN'S CUP RACE

It's been called a "dash across Lake Michigan", an eighty mile drag race between a party in Wisconsin and a party in Michigan. Milwaukee's South Shore Yacht Club's annual Fourth of July weekend Queen's Cup race.

In addition to the thrill of racing aboard a GL70, I enjoyed watching the give and take of many Nedeau family members in action. Although, the Nedeau family has the most family members racing on a GL70 regularly, most of the boats also have some of the skipper's family members involved.

As you can see, we had a big crew for the Queen's Cup Race. After an extremely slow start and light air all night, the following morning brought a 12 knot breeze which we rode on the rhumbline for five hours while crossing the finish line ahead of POROROCA and one-half hour ahead of WINDQUEST on corrected time.

2007 CHICAGO NOOD REGATTA

Jack's Recollection of the race:
"Going into the Chicago NOOD Regatta, PIED PIPER had made a lot of changes to the boat and sails, which needed to be sorted out. Over the winter, we changed our deck layout adding clutches to the spinnaker guys and spinnaker sheets. This allowed

Place	#	Boat Name	Owner	R 1	R 2	R 3	R 4	Total
1	18970	Nitemare	Tom Neill	1	1	1	1	4
2	41104	Pied Piper	Jack Jennings	2	5	2	2	11
3	70	Evolution	Peter Reichelsd orfer	3	2	3	3	11
4	52701	Windance r	Johh/Sam Nedeau	4	6	4	4	18
5	28115	Mirage	Rick Woodwort h	5	4	7	5	21
6	77984	Pororoca	Gene McCarthy Bob Zeman	6	3	6	7	22
7	87666	Thirsty Tiger	Bert D'Ottavio	7	7	5	6	25

2007 Chicago NOOD Regatta results.

the spinnakers to be trimmed on the primary winch at all times (more horse power than the smaller winches). We also began to experiment with the rig tension and new sail designs which all needed to be tested. We built a new asymmetric spinnaker and a new main sail which was an improvement on the previous generation. We also added three new upwind head sails to the inventory. Running rigging was improved with the intention of increasing durability, decreasing weight aloft and accommodating the handling of both symmetric and asymmetric spinnakers.

We had also added some new team members who brought a lot of good experience and ability to the boat. Dave Lamere came aboard and did a great job fitting in, working the mast and foredeck with Dave Jochum. In the back of the boat, Mike Hoey came aboard in a tactical role working with Ron Sherry. Prior to the regatta, we had three great days of practice sailing, but unfortunately, when race day finally came, we were left with little or no wind and postponements.

While waiting for the wind to build, we provided some entertainment for the fleet. Ben Biddick and Mike Hoey put clown noses on and invented the new sport of bunk boarding. They removed the bunks from the boat, threw them in the water

(thankfully they floated) and
used them as surf boards.
We towed them behind
the boat at a speed of nine
knots. With two boards being
towed, it quickly became
a competition to see who
could outlast the other, as

Stu Thompson, Trimmer.   Mike Rehe, Trimmer.

both surfers tried to push each other off his board. The most
tactical dual came between Dave Lamere and Ron Sherry who
used several different moves to try and upset the other's balance
including head fakes, arm grabs and leg kicks. Eric Vigrass added
to the fun by head-butting a turning mark as we motored past.

Perry Lewis even got in on the act swimming over in his best
speedo from a rival boat to try out the bunk boards. For the final
act, Ben Biddick, Mike Rehe and Eric Jochum formed a three-man
pyramid as we motored through the fleet. Not much sailing was
accomplished, but good laughs were had by all.

Only four races were held over the three-day Chicago NOOD
Regatta, one on Friday, one on Saturday and two on Sunday. On
Friday, we worked to start near the pin and headed to the left.
This seemed to be working well and we tacked to port to cross
NITEMARE and stay in touch with the rest of the fleet. The
wind was real touch and go and NITEMARE pushed further to
the left almost to the port layline and then tacked. This tactic
allowed her to lead into the weather mark. We rounded very
closely behind EVOLUTION. In the light wind, we set our 1.5
asymmetric spinnaker. It was interesting to see how it performed
and we quickly found in wind speeds under seven knots, it was
not our most effective sail. NITEMARE did a good job of
protecting her position. We crossed gibes with EVOLUTION
and were able to get inside overlap at the leeward mark where
we executed a great Mexican take-down. This effectively forced

EVOLUTION to round the mark outside of us, putting them behind us. NITEMARE sailed this race better than the rest and finished first with us a close second boat-for-boat, but not on corrected time. The light wind and flat water made it difficult for us to leg out and use our boat speed. We have worked hard to make the boat more competitive in under eight knots of wind, but she is nothing special in those conditions. Because of this, we have to sail very well in order to have a good result.

Saturday was much the same with light winds. We actually rounded the first weather mark in first place, only to give it up on the downwind leg, falling into a light wind patch and sailing through the wind shadows of some smaller boats which limited our speed. NITEMARE slipped past and won the second race. By the end of Race 2, based upon corrected time, we were in fifth place.

Sunday brought a little better breeze and the race committee was able to get two races completed. Because of the light air, the race courses were again set with relatively short distances with legs under two miles in length. It was tough to leg out away from our competitors. NITEMARE did the best job of starting near the pin and then heading to the left side of the course. She sailed as fast as possible for the majority of the leg while the rest of the fleet jockeyed with each other in the middle of the course. We managed to take two second place finishes on Sunday. NITEMARE ran away with the regatta by placing first in all four races. We tied on points with EVOLUTION and won the tie breaker which put us in second place."

As you can see in the 2007 Bayview Mackinac Race Results chart on page 115, NITEMARE won with EVOLUTION in second place and WINDANCER in third. It was an even lighter air race than the Chicago Mackinac Race conducted one week earlier. In this race, NITEMARE won without the need for any handicapping. It was a great duel between NITEMARE and EVOLUTION coming down to the finish line located across from Mission Point

2007 Bayview Mackinac Race
Current Standings as of
Friday, 27/Jul/2007 @ 03:51pm

L 70 Class

Sail	Boat	Rating	City, State	Rounding Time	Finish Time	Elapsed Time	Corrected	
USA 18970	Nitemare	1.308	Berkeley, IL		Monday - 05:25:11	39:15:11	51:20:34	1
USA 70	Evolution	1.322	Sheboygan, WI	Monday - 00:00	Monday - 05:26:06	39:16:06	51:54:45	2
USA 52701	Windancer	1.316	North Muskegon, MI		Monday - 06:37:06	40:27:06	53:14:03	3
USA 28115	Mirage	1.305	Northbrook, IL		Monday - 07:00:06	40:50:06	53:17:22	4
USA 25168	Stripes	1.308	Ann Arbor, MI		Monday - 07:01:56	40:51:56	53:27:07	5
USA 50045	TBD	1.315	Harriso n Township, MI		Monday - 06:54:07	40:44:07	53:34:00	6
USA 77984	Pororoca	1.304	Chicago, IL	Sunday - 16:10	Monday - 07:16:17	41:06:17	53:36:02	7
USA 41104	Pied Piper	1.319	Niles , IL		Monday - 06:59:21	40:49:21	53:50:41	8
USA 97503	Chance	1.309	Kohler, WI	Sunday - 19:50			Retired	9
USA 87666	Thirsty Tiger	1.310	Joliet, IL	Sunday - 22:05			Retired	10

Resort on the island. NITEMARE finished only fifty-five seconds ahead of EVOLUTION. PIED PIPER actually finished fifth, but ended up in eighth place with handicapping.

Jack's recollection of the race:

"We had a pretty good start on the pin end of the line. The other boats bunched up to weather of us. We got our nose out at the start and went fast. During the day, it was breezy (between ten and twenty knots) and we extended our lead on the fleet throughout the day. Dusk began approaching later in the evening. At one point during this time, we actually closed on the much faster boat, EQUATION, which had started in the group ahead of us.

About 1:00 a.m. Saturday night, I came on watch and saw that NITEMARE was on our hip at about 100 degrees and 1/4 to 1/2 mile back. At that time, it appeared we were, once again, leading the fleet. The wind slowed and swung around 180 degrees. We could see the rest of the fleet coming up on our side and some of them got outside of us where there appeared to be better air.

Three new sailors became part of our crew in this race. They were Kevin Savitt, Adam Hollerback and Brian Smith (whose photo appears in the Bay Harbor Regatta story.)

Adam Hollerback, trimmer.

Kevin Savitt, Grinder.

When day broke Sunday morning, we were in a bad spot and had fallen behind during the night. We were too close to shore and tried to jibe further out in lake before approaching the turning mark. We were so far behind the leaders that we found ourselves in the company of North American 40s and other 40-footers, which under most conditions, would not be alongside a GL70 this late in the race.

NITEMARE and EVOLUTION were further up the race course at that time. We could see we were behind STRIPES and far behind MIRAGE. For us, it became a race between our three boats. Our course, after rounding, was basically five miles off shore and five miles west of the rhumbline.

We raced all through Sunday night and found at sunrise on Monday morning that we were next to STRIPES and MIRAGE was a little behind us. We were now in the Straits of Mackinac heading for the finish line. The lead changed more than once during this stretch. The competition was fierce in light air with each competitor plainly in sight of the others.

Terry Kohler (left) with John Nedeau after the 2007 Bayview Mackinac Race.

I remember that, even though we were not going to do well in the race, the crew sailed with a lot of pride and wanted to beat MIRAGE and STRIPES across the line. It was fairly tricky coming into the finish with patchy wind. Eric Vigrass was driving the boat and he was doing a really nice job. So, I let him drive through to the finish. Sometimes, if the driver is doing well, it's better to let him continue rather than switch out the helmsman. J.B. Shumaker was trimming the main and Adam Hollerbach was trimming the jib. Towards the end, Brian Smith took over for J.B. as he had been trimming since dawn.

We got a lift at the end and crossed forty-five seconds ahead of MIRAGE and two minutes ahead of STRIPES. It was a good feeling coming from being behind both boats at the turning mark and still prevailing at the finish.

In future distance races, I think we need to interpret weather forecasts better than we have in the past. Also,

Peter Reichelsdorfer (right) presenting the 2007 Offshore Trophy to Tom Neill of NITEMARE.

under light air conditions, it is sometimes a disadvantage
to be in the lead. If you sail into a hole with no air, the
boats coming up from behind can see your predicament
and avoid that area. It surely happened in this race."

Because this was the second and final Mackinac race of the 2007
season, The Great Lakes 70 Association held its annual Mackinac
Island party for everyone involved in the GL70 fleet. The good
camaraderie that existed between these veteran competitors was
evident everywhere. Pictured on page 117 after the Bayview
Mackinac Race are second place and third place skippers, Terry
Kohler, EVOLUTION (left) and John Nedeau of WINDANCER.

Also, at the same party, the annual GL70 Offshore Trophy was
awarded (photo above) to Tom Neill, owner of NITEMARE
on the left. The award is made to Tom by Peter Reichelsdorfer
on the right. Although all the owners did their utmost to finish
the Mackinac Races ahead of Tom, he and his crew prevailed
in both events. Nonetheless, they universally admired his grit for
campaigning his boat as hard as he did while being seriously ill.

2007 BAY HARBOR REGATTA

BOAT NAME	Bay Harbor GL70 Regatta				
	RACE 1	RACE 2	RACE 3	RACE4	TOTAL
PIED PIPER	6	1	1	1	9
EVOLUTION	1	2	3	3	9
BLOW EM TO SMITHEREENS	5	4	2	2	13
MIRAGE	3	3	4	5	15
POROROCA	2	6	6	6	20
THIRSTY TIGER	7	7	5	4	23
WINDANCER	4	5	7	7	23

Jack's Recollection of the Regatta:

"This was a two-day event with five races scheduled. We set out
on Thursday morning in a very weak breeze. We had a good
start at the pin end of the line at better than full speed. The wind
continued to get lighter as the race progressed. We came out of the
left hand side of the first upwind beat out of position. We rounded
the mark in third place and worked our way downwind. This race
really got turned upside down as the last downwind leg featured
boats sailing the downwind leg to the finish with jibs up and going
up wind as the wind fought to fill in from a new direction. There
were many opportunities to pass boats and also fall behind because
the pressure was so sporadic and the wind direction kept shifting.

Ron Sherry, our tactician, was really tough on himself and
feeling a little responsible for sailing us out of some new pressure
on the last downwind leg. The best thing about sailing with Ron is
that he is his own toughest critic and while he may make a mistake,
he rarely makes two in row. We finished the race in sixth place out
of eight boats in race one. The good news is that we had two more
races scheduled for the day and were ready to bounce back.

Brian Smith from Quantum, Newport, RI, and former main
trimmer aboard the GL70 Holua, had also come onboard for
the week to trim the main He was a good addition. Dave Shriner
continued to work on mast tuning and set up. We lengthened
the headstay about two inches and felt really fast upwind in the

Ron Sherry, Tactician.

Brian Smith, Trimmer.

subsequent two races with more mast rake in the flat water. After a short postponement, the afternoon sea breeze began to fill in.

In the second race, we again started near the pin with good speed. We lead the entire way and finally recorded a first place finish. This was a great relief because, up until this point, we had not put any bullets on the board for the entire season. Sailing the boat in flat water and moderate breeze was great. You can sail very close to the wind and make nice smooth tacks and gibes. This was the fastest the boat felt all year and it seemed that our tuning set up and practice time were starting to pay off. We went on to win the last race of the day, again leading from start to finish.

After the first day's racing, we were sitting in second place, two points out of first. EVOLUTION had sailed very consistently and was leading the regatta. We felt, with any type of breeze tomorrow, we would be in good shape to win the event. Day two came and, unfortunately, we were postponed at the dock due to lack of wind. This left only time for one race on Friday. Even if we did win the last race, there was a good chance that we would not be able to gain two points on them in one race. On the way out to the starting area, we talked about trying to force EVOLUTION back into the fleet while limiting their options to make a clean start. If possible, this could enable us to escape and make up the points we needed. If the opportunity presented itself we were going to take it.

As it turned out in the prestart, we were able to chase EVOLUTION passed the pin end of the starting line and block any attempt she made to get back to the line. Mike Hoey and Dave Jochum were big assets here as they did a great job communicating the position of the other boat and the next move we needed to make. EVOLUTION was stuck and forced to follow us across the starting line behind the rest of the fleet. We then started trying to pick our way through the fleet and tacked away from EVOLUTION. We were able to sail through the entire fleet and finished the race in first, passing BLOW 'EM TO SMITHEREENS on the last upwind leg right near the weather mark. EVOLUTION had also done a good job working through the fleet. We finished in first with EVOLUTION placing third, good enough to tie on points, with us winning the tie breaker with three first place finishes.

2007 VERVE CUP REGATTA

One Design Division									
GL 70									
1.	USA 41104	Pied Piper	Jack Jennings	1	1	1	1	4.0
2.	USA 28115	Mirage	Mirage Group	2	5	3	2	12.0
3.	USA 18970	Nitemare	Tom Neill	3	3	2	5	13.0
4.	USA 70	Evolution	Kohler/Reichelsdorfer	4	2	4	3	13.0
5.	USA 87666	Thirsty Tiger	Albert D'Ottavio	7	4	5	4	20.0
6.	USA 52701	Windancer	John Nedeau	5	6	7	6	24.0
7.	USA 77984	Pororoca	McCarthy/Zeman	6	7	6	7	26.0

Jack's Recollection of the race:

Race 1

The 2007 Verve Cup was the culmination of a lot of work the core members of the PIED PIPER team had put in for the past two years. There were only four races sailed. We had a picture perfect day on Friday with a northwest breeze in the 12 to 16 knot range. It was clear from the get-go that the fleet was going to be shooting for us in this regatta after our good results in Bay Harbor. In the pre-start of race one, WINDANCER and EVOLUTION tacked very close to our lee bow while NITEMARE came rolling in from our weather hip. Shortly after the start, we tacked to port to escape the bad air from this pack of boats sailing tightly together. We had been the first boat on the race course that morning and had been favoring the right middle area of the course. While the fleet pushed left we sailed the right middle into a nice right hand shift and tacked to the lifted board. The waves were a little more head on, when sailing on port tack so it was harder keeping the boat on her numbers. There was a fair amount of distance between us and the group that had headed to the left. First we crossed NITEMARE, then MIRAGE and then EVOLUTION. We were close to the layline so we held on port while the rest of the boats tacked on our hip. We waited for a good spot to tack back onto starboard and rounded the mark in first and lead the rest of the race.

Race 2
EVOLUTION again tried to line up to leeward of us, but they didn't get her bow out far enough to cause us any problem coming off the starting line. We sailed on starboard for as long as we wanted until we had a clear lane to head to the right middle of the course, which is where we wanted to position ourselves. We lead that race from start to finish. In race two, we were the only boat to use a #2 headsail. Most of the other boats chose a #3 jib, which I felt gave us an advantage in the first beat because we sailed higher and faster.

Race 3
We had our best start at the pin which was favored because the last shift had been to the left. With 30 seconds until the gun, the pin was wide open and we gave ourselves plenty of runway to make sure that we didn't end up over the line or at the pin to soon. When the gun went off, the rest of the fleet was pointing at our transom. EVOLUTION tacked first to port and then we covered shortly thereafter. We lead this race start to finish as well.

Race 4

This was a mid-distance race of roughly 30 miles covering all
different points of sail. One difference in this race from last year's
mid-distance race is that the GL70s would be the last start and
we would end up racing through all the slower boats as the race
progressed. At the start, we were called over the line early and
had to restart the boat. The first leg was an upwind course to
the mark. We started working our way upwind behind the fleet.
The first mark was a mess of big, little and middle sized boats
all moving at very different speeds. Despite the disadvantage of
a restart, we rounded the mark overlapped with the two leading
GL70s NITEMARE and MIRAGE. The next leg was a reach and
we set our asymmetric spinnaker, which seemed to perform fairly
well as we reached along in moderate breeze in Lake Michigan's
lumpy sea conditions. The sail was steadier than her symmetric
counterparts and we were able to gain an advantage. The wind
continued to get lighter as we headed to the next turning mark and
NITEMARE remained close astern. They would get a puff and
overlap us and then we would get a puff and move a little ahead.
When we rounded the leeward mark and headed back
upwind the boats had all closed distance to each other. THIRSTY
TIGER had made a move and she rounded the mark in first
place. We came into the mark with inside overlap and starboard
advantage on NITEMARE and EVOLUTION. We had a bit of
a debacle with sail change at the mark rounding. I think we had a
communication error from the back of the boat to the front. The
chute came down late without the jib being up in time. The crew
managed to sort out the issue pretty quickly and we were going
without any loss in race position. As we worked back upwind, we
were able to get past THIRSTY TIGER while NITEMARE lost
pace and fell off to leeward. EVOLUTION was moving pretty well
and took the lead as we tacked away.

The next leg was a jib reach with a spinnaker reach to the finish. Getting around this last upwind mark would be important to have clear air. The boats were almost bow-to-bow. EVOLUTION, just coming out of a tack, was at a disadvantage because she had to build speed. We were able to put her in our wind shadow before reaching the mark. It's a good feeling watching your competition lose speed as you continue to advance.

The wind continued to build as we rounded the mark and bore off on a close reach. As we made it to the last turning mark and headed to the finish, it looked like we would be able to carry the A-Sail on the last leg to the finish. I was a little hesitant because the wind was gusting up to 20 knots and the North Sails code 1.5 was only really supposed to be used in a max of 15 knots. We were excited to put it up and see how the boat would perform. We knew the shape would be good for the conditions and true wind angle. The only concern was whether material used in the sail would be strong enough. Since it was close to the end of the year, we set the sail and off we went.

With the A-sail flying, the boat was moving at a steady ten knots and up to 13 knots in the puffs. There were still a fair amount of smaller boats in our area heading for the finish, so we picked our way through them. EVOLUTION did not have an A-sail capable of being effectively used in this wind range and we opened up our lead. It was a good feeling heading towards the Chicago Skyline with the whole crew hiking hard on the aft weather rail. We crossed the finish line first and won the race on corrected time as well.

2007 GL70 SEASON FINAL STANDINGS

This chart shows the finishing positions for the entire 2007 racing season. Each boat was allowed to throw out three races when calculating its final point total. NITEMARE finished two points ahead of EVOLUTION, followed by PIED PIPER, who won the last seven races of the season, finishing in third place.

BOAT NAME	POINTS	THROW	TOTAL
NITEMARE	67	33	34
EVOLUTION	45	9	36
PIED PIPER	79	30	49
MIRAGE	75	17	58
POROROCA	86	21	65
WINDANCER	113	27	86
THIRSTY TIGER	122	30	92
BLOW EM TO SMITHEREENS	140	33	107
STRIPES	159	33	126
CHANCE	183	33	150

MEET THE SAILORS

The Crew of WINDANCER just after their third place finish in the 2007 Bayview to Mackinac Race.

PIED PIPER
Jack Jennings-Skipper

Jack Jennings lived his early years in Evanston, Illinois. He moved to Chicago to live with his father during his high school years attending Loyola Academy. He enjoyed playing basketball and the competitive nature of the sport. He was very focused on playing, but,even though he practiced every day he failed to make his high school team. In the summer months he would also sail on his dad's racing yacht, PIED PIPER.

He began his sailing career when he was 12 years old. Like many aspiring young sailors, he received his earliest training in the junior sailing program offered by Burnham Park Yacht Club near where the PIED PIPER was docked. Two years later, his dad, Dick Jennings, a well-known yacht racer on the international circuit, bought a Creekmore 22. A keel boat, it was rigged with a main, jib and spinnaker. Jack took on the most difficult task aboard a racing boat, foredeck. While racing with his dad, they had a lot of success with the Creekmore 22, which was named TERMITE.

At the age of 14, Jack sailed in his first overnight race aboard his dad's GL70, PIED PIPER. It was the annual Queen's Cup night race across Lake Michigan from Milwaukee, Wisconsin to Grand Haven, Michigan. His biggest memory was how bored he felt sitting on the rail all night on a jib reach. He did, however, begin to appreciate the talents of Jamie Schwarz, who served as bowman/captain on PIED PIPER, and was the jib trimmer aboard TERMITE. Jamie was extremely knowledgeable and moved quickly around the deck to execute all the tasks required of the foredeck position under trying conditions.

Jamie maintained the boat in immaculate condition and was meticulous in preparing for major sailing events. He always worked harder and slept less than anyone else onboard—and he expected everyone else to match his work ethic. Later that year, Jack helped deliver the big boat to various racing venues and recalls his first Bayview Mackinac Race in the summer of 1994. He remembers being very excited about the huge crowds lining the Black River in downtown Port Huron as **PIED PIPER** and the other GL70s made their way up to the starting line three miles out into Lake Huron

In 1995, during his first Chicago to Mackinac Race, Jack experienced what every sailor dreads, a dismasting offshore. On the first day, **PIED PIPER** was sailing about 25 miles off-shore on port tack when in the early evening hours a storm began building from the west. The crew knew the storm was on its way and were flying their main and a #4 jib. The storm hit with driving rain and 60 mph winds. The GL70 uses running backstays to help support the middle sections of the mast, which are similar to the running rigging for a spinnaker with a block mounted aft, leading to a winch further forward.

During a gust, estimated at 65 mph, the portside runner block shackle broke, which caused the middle of the mast to lurch forward. This sudden load on the winch broke it out of the deck and sent it hurling upward and into the upper portion of the mast. The mast broke in three sections, near the tip, halfway down and on the deck. The mast, boom and both sails fell over the starboard side of the boat. There was also the threat of the underwater mast poking a hole in the hull. The crew moved quickly and pulled the pins on all the stays supporting the mast. After 20 minutes, which seemed like an eternity, all the pins were out and the mast and sails fell away from the boat and began descending 200 feet to the bottom of Lake Michigan.

For the entire crew and especially for a 15-year-old on his first Chicago Mackinac Race, it was an eye-opening experience. Luckily, no one was hurt. The engine was engaged and they motored to Waukegan, IL, docked the boat and some of the crew took the train back to Chicago. Obviously, the 1995 racing season for **PIED PIPER** had come to an abrupt close. Despite this ominous introduction to offshore racing, Jack has never missed a Mackinac Race since.

When Jack was 18, he worked the foredeck aboard **PIED PIPER** during another Chicago Mackinac Race. On the first night, the order was given to jibe the boat. The GL70 has an aluminum reaching strut attached to the mast. Jack was working to disconnect the reaching strut so it could be moved to the port side when Jamie suddenly swung the strut over thinking it was already disconnected. This action trapped Jack's thumb between the mast and the strut, crushing it. It caused incredible pain, but while offshore nothing could be done except to apply first aid and sail on. They used a plastic spoon as a splint for the remaining 30 hours of the race. When the race was over, Jack had to go directly to the doctor and have his hand put into a cast.

The following weekend, **PIED PIPER** was racing again on Lake Michigan against the other GL70s in the annual Bay Harbor Regatta. Jack was not pleased with their results after the first race and vocalized this to his dad. Jack's dad, not being one to take criticism lightly, suggested Jack either put up or shut up. "If you think you can do it better, take the helm," he told Jack. So Jack had his turn at the helm for the second race, cast and all. **PIED PIPER** started the race at the committee boat end slightly behind. They tacked to port and gained from a right hand wind shift that allowed **PIED PIPER** to cross the fleet as they came back on starboard.

Jack had one of the Caribbean's best sailors, Howard Palmer, onboard. Howard had won many races in the Caribbean on his Dubois 42 racer named **IMMIGRANT**. Howard did a great job of reading the wind, keeping the boat in phase with the wind shifts. It really helped to be in the lead early as **PIED PIPER** was able to lead the rest of the race. It was Jack's first time at the helm of the big boat and he walked away with a victory.

Because he could no longer work the foredeck the rest of the season with his thumb in a cast, he learned the important job of trimming, which is vital for any sailor who wants to be competitive. He finished that season with the cast still on. The doctor had made Jack's cast so that he could still grab a line, allowing him to become the trimmer of the starboard primary. Opposite Jack, on the port primary, was a terrific Midwest sailor named Brian Torresen, who was also the yard manager for Torresen Marine where PIED PIPER was stored in the winter. Jack learned a lot about jib trim from watching Brian. The overlapping jibs on PIED PIPER require not so much strength, but technique and hand speed to tack properly. Jack's dad would usually drive from the leeward side of the boat, which is somewhat of an unorthodox method. However this position did allow him to keep an eye on the jib trim so if Jack did make an error, his dad was the first to let him know. Sometimes this "coaching" made the Monday after racing a bit rough but Jack did improve because of the constant feedback from his dad. Plus, it gave Jack a thick skin that would help him later in his sailing.

Jack admits that yacht racing satisfies his love of competition. He also likes the autonomy of being on his own boat with lots of freedom and a great sense of adventure, which is always a part of every race. He was also drawn to the sport by the great group of people his dad had assembled as part of the PIED PIPER Racing Team. They were all living a dream, were successful in their lives outside of sailing and were a true team.

During these years, he had graduated from high school and attended Ripon College in Ripon, Wisconsin. He continued pursuing the sport of basketball and did make the JV team. During these college years, he spent a lot more time at the helm of PIED PIPER during distance races.

One of Jack's greatest memories of a Chicago Mackinac Race was during the 1996 race when they were becalmed off Milwaukee with the other GL70s. After being parked for some time, the boats around them began getting puffs and pulling away from them. Because PIED PIPER could not reach the puffs available to all the other boats, the crew found themselves in last place with the unenviable position of following the fleet around the course, resulting in a possible last place finish. His dad and Paul Snow, PIED PIPER's long-time navigator, were down at the navigation station plotting a course, which would take them on a more direct route to Mackinac Island outside the Manitou Islands. He knew all the other boats were taking the normal easterly route through the Manitou Islands and then north to Mackinac. From their location, it would be a 160-mile trip to the Manitous.

By daylight on Monday morning, they had leapfrogged the whole fleet and were in the lead. But as they sailed under the Mackinac Bridge their wind died. Their pursuers, larger and faster yachts by design, were in better air and were gaining quickly. As the other boats neared, PIED PIPER got just enough breeze to finish 15 minutes in the lead for a dramatic first-to-finish. It was the boat's sixth first-to-finish. No other boat in the history of the Chicago Mac Race has finished first more often than PIED PIPER.

The 1999 Chicago Mackinac Race was a great year for PIED PIPER as it was the overall winner. The race began with a 20 knot upwind start. With Dick Jennings at the wheel and great sail trimming, they sailed higher and faster than everyone else the first night and won with a five mile margin. On distance races, they sail with a smaller crew and need people who can do more than one job. They used four or five helmsman on that race.

Jack graduated from Ripon College in April of 2002, immediately flew to Miami and began working for a friend, John Schiefer. John had a business cleaning the bottom of boats and Jack worked for eight months as a diver cleaning boat hulls while they were in the water. This periodic cleaning is necessary for any boats in salt water.

During a visit to Chicago, he had dinner with his dad and his friend, Ken Campia. Ken was the owner of a 74-foot boat called RENAISSANCE which was lying in Palma, Majorca, Spain. He was looking for a crew to sail the boat to the island of Antigua. Dick suggested to Jack that it could be a great experience sailing across the Atlantic Ocean.

Jack decided he wanted to go and interviewed with the captain of the boat, Peter Pexton. After the interview, Peter gave Jack the opportunity to join the crew for the delivery. He joined the boat in Palma, Majorca.

After spending three days walking around the beautiful island, Jack and Renaissance were ready to cast off. Jack was the only American aboard. The captain, the first mate and the first mate's brother were from South Africa. The cook was from Great Britain and the balance of the crew was comprised of an Aussie and a native of Palma. Jack stood a regular watch at the helm and plotted positions to keep an eye on the boat's course. Their first stop was the Straits of Gibraltar. Jack was amazed with his ability to see across the Straits into North Africa. From there, it was five days to the Canary Islands for provisioning and three weeks at sea before reaching Antigua. They sailed in the trade winds and enjoyed warm weather, wearing shorts with ten to 15 knot breezes all the way. While on that crossing, Jack celebrated his 22nd birthday in the exact middle of the Atlantic Ocean.

In January 2005, Jack also sailed his first Key West Race Week as a skipper with his Melges 24, placing 25th out of 60 boats. He sailed his second Ft. Lauderdale to Jamaica Race onboard EQUATION and at the end of February 2005, he was invited to try out for a crew position aboard ABN AMRO TWO, which would be competing in The Volvo Ocean Race. This around-the-world race was only conducted once every four years. ABN AMRO, a Dutch bank, was entering two similar boats in the race. ABN AMRO ONE would be crewed by professionals. ABN AMRO TWO would be crewed by a few professionals and mostly amateurs from various countries including the U.S. Out of one thousand applicants, Jack was one of five selected to go into the final round of the competition in Portugal in March 2005. He missed the final cut by one person.

PIED PIPER
Ben Biddick-Boat Captain/Grinder

Here is Ben's sailing biography in his own words:

"My first sailing experience was with my parents. I have no idea as to what kind of boat it was, but I remember that they were always introducing me to new experiences and adventures.

Thereafter, I can remember being taught to sail at Camp Daggett in northern Michigan. This experience was hell, to say the least. The night before our first sail, the counselors told us ghost stories around the fire. One story involved a past camper who had a sleepwalking disorder and who walked in front of a large cross in the camp at midnight and just plain disappeared. From then on, his spirit would haunt the cabin he had been in; rattling the doors because the counselors didn't lock the door at night. Needless to say, there was a lot of crying nine and ten-year-old campers that night.

The following day was sailing. We were divided into groups of three or four and put out on boats. The only instructions were: "This is the mainsheet and the tiller. Go have fun." We had no idea what we were doing and, with three other just as inexperienced sailors, we were basically adrift. One girl, I remember, cried the whole time, which didn't help the others. After being out there for a while, we started to float towards the cross, the same one that would make you disappear. Now almost everyone was starting to panic and scream. Welcome to sailing, Ben.

I didn't sail much. I was always playing hockey all year-round. So, there was no junior sailing program for me. My first competitive sailing experience was the Red Fox. (Charlevoix Yacht Club's annual Red Fox Regatta is now a Labor Day tradition for sailors from all over the Great Lakes.)

I was on the mighty TERMITE, owned by Dick Jennings, which was sitting in the shed with PIED PIPER in Muskegon, MI. Jamie, Dick's previous 'go-to-guy,' was running the show with his two girlfriends and me. We won the Red Fox both years that we entered. It was beginner's luck, I suppose, but I was stoked.

After that, I started to get into sailing more and researched different boats. I have always been fascinated with multi-hulls and bought a 16' Hobie Cat from the Lake Charlevoix Mariners at an auction for $250.00, which I worked off. I sailed that for a couple years in the same condition I bought it; sun-faded-classic Hobie yellow and in sore shape. Later, I started to get the itch and my father and I restored it back to a pristine condition, painting it and replacing the trampoline.

Several summers ago, Dick Jennings asked my dad if I was available to work for him in the summer down in Chicago. I was neither ready nor mature enough to take on that role the first time around, but the following summer I signed up. I had no idea what I was getting into, nor did I have any idea of what I would eventually be capable of doing. I remember asking my dad how I was going to be able to do this since I didn't have any experience. He said, "Don't worry about a thing, you'll be just fine." And I was.

Now I'm responsible for the upkeep and maintenance of a Santa Cruz 70. Who would have known?

Primarily, my racing experience has been limited to PIED PIPER (SC70 and Melges 24) or in the Red Fox Regatta, as mentioned above. I do, however, have a fond memory of the first time I was aboard Piper and the wind was on. I felt as if we were riding a giant bull. I yelled, "YeeeHaaww!" I continued to do it at the beginning of each new season the first time the boat really took off.

I also remember this year's (2007) tacking duel in the Harbor Springs Regatta. Kevin Savitt and I were slamming away at the grinder pedals as we continued covering BLOW 'EM TO SMITHEREENS (the boat previously named COLT 45). I lost track of how many tacks we did, but I think we hit about five tacks in ten minutes or so. Talk about a workout, but I loved it.

My other claim-to-fame was the Maxi Yacht Rolex Cup, to which I was invited in Sardinia, Italy. Mike Hoey was kind enough to think of me when the team was being formed. The end result was the experience of a lifetime, one that couldn't justly be described here. I can tell you, though, that grinding on PIPER is nothing compared to the power that Chippewa has. Imagine four grinders unable to move the pedals in second gear. And the sound of the jib-sheet pinging as it was brought in on the massive 18"+ drum; kind of scary at first. Other races don't stick out in my mind so much, but more so the camaraderie formed from the experience and the friends I have made along the way.

Sailing on PIPER has definitely had its ups and downs for me. I don't have a good frame of reference to compare to another program, but I can tell you that we run a tight ship. If things aren't clicking like they should, we tighten our belts and buckle down in order to bring the pace back up. I like the driving, competitive force that's built into our team. All in all, you couldn't ask for a better opportunity and experience. I'm very thankful to be a major part of PIED PIPER Racing."

PIED PIPER
Brian Brophy-Mast

Brian Brophy, a PIED PIPER crewmember from 1982 until the present tells his story:

"I began sailing at an early age. Growing up in a small town without immediate access to lakes or rivers, it may be surprising that I have been so involved in the sport. Joliet, Illinois is located on the Illinois Sanitary canal and I did see some watercraft passing from time to time. Once I saw a large boat with the mast on the deck heading north, most likely to Lake Michigan. I did dream of sailing on the big lake some day. I remember in high school meeting a girlfriend's father who had sailing magazines. The stories I read about the America's Cup sailors and how they were treated like Princes in the Castles of Marblehead inspired me to wonder if I might be a part of that world some day.

My parents belonged to a pool club when I was young and after the summer I began swimming lessons at the Joliet YMCA. I liked the water and felt accomplished as I rose through the levels of skill and endurance. Being a good swimmer, I took all the boating classes and liked sailing the most. Later, I met Vincent Alferi, an attorney, his friends and crewmembers aboard the C&C 39', KINGS COURIER. After an afternoon and a couple of evening sails with them, I was asked to join the crew for the Chicago to Mackinac Race in 1977. These obviously social sailors were good men and good crewmates.

My first race was eventful in every way, especially the termination of the voyage. After sailing through a few squalls and doldrums, the KINGS COURIER found her lines on Monday morning as we began to broad reach through Gray's Reef and beat to the bridge. As I would come to find out, the last few miles can be the most treacherous and fluky.

As evening came and we agonizingly strained to get to the bridge, we ran aground on Graham's South Shoal. We tried many tactics to free ourselves from the muck by extending the crew out on the boom and even winching the anchor in. That was my job, to swim the anchor out into the Straits and drop it to the lake floor. I was exhausted after the fourth try and must have passed out for a short while. I vaguely remember the Coast Guard Launch finally freeing us in the foggy night. I awoke the next morning to the sight of a beautiful island with a blue sky, the sweet clanging of halyards and the smell of the island's main transportation by-product. I was hooked and determined to finish the race some day, completely!

After I graduated in December of 1980, I traveled to Florida to find out how good I was by trying to get on a Southern Ocean Racing Circuit (SORC) Boat. I met with success when I gave my information to Kevin Thompson, skipper of a One Ton Fractional rigged named, BELLY UP. I had a great time and many adventures on this, my only SORC regatta. I met sailors from around the world and began to forge a friendship with some of the LOUISIANA CRUDE crew that included Billy Wagner and Andy McCormick. This was when I met Dick Jennings for the first time.

After returning to the Midwest I married and bounced around for the balance of the summer on various yachts. Eventually joined the delivery crew for a Peterson 43,' PIED PIPER which was owned by Dick Jennings. I worked my way onto the regular Chicago crew and made my first Mac Race with Dick in 1983. That was a big step to make a trip with a contending boat. The guys were a riot and Dick was a master of managing the crew and the boat. I had a great time and I guess that I was accepted as well. I have made every Chicago Mac Race since then with Dick and the PIED PIPER boats.

We shattered a 76-year-old Mackinac speed record by over five hours in 1987. On that race, I wore an armband with my father's initials on it the whole time. I did this to honor the first anniversary of his death. When I finished the race in 1986, I found out at the dock my father had passed away the evening of July 25th, the first night out on that year's Mac race. Looking back later that summer, I recalled being hoisted to the top of the mast that night and how clear the sky was. There was an issue with the halyards to correct and it was my position to do all the 'above deck' work. I have told only a few mates this but, while untangling the mess, I had to disconnect my harness to make the halyards fair. I wonder if, in that instant, I had a little help, but did not know it at the time."

PIED PIPER
Tom Ervin-Halyards/Author

PIED PIPER RACING
PIED-PIPER.COM

From time to time over the years, I have been involved in my favorite sport, sailing. My first sailboat was a 14' wooden boat which had a hole in the bottom. Whenever my brother and I heard small craft warnings on the radio, we would jump in the car and drive to the boat, which resided in a small creek off Lake St. Clair outside Detroit, MI. We knew the small craft warnings meant we would catch a great breeze. One of us would sail while the other would bail. My next boat was a CAL 25, which I kept at Keane's Marina in downtown Detroit. After a couple of years of great fun on this boat, the kids began to come along and my sailing days were over until 1999, when, as a 58-year-old, I revisited the sport of my youth.

My great adventures in the 2005 Bayview Mackinac race aboard the J105, VENOM and the 2007 Chicago to Mackinac Race aboard the GL70, PIED PIPER were extremely rewarding for me on many mental and emotional levels. With these two experiences, I've learned it's never too late to reach for your dreams. It is my sincerest hope that you, the reader, will consider pursuing your dreams and goals with a renewed sense of enthusiasm and purpose.

PIED PIPER
Mike Hoey-Paramedic/Watch Captain

Mike Hoey, one of the watch captains, began racing sailboats at the age of eight on Lake St. Clair, the connector lake between Lake Huron and Lake Erie. Bob Orr, a neighbor, recruited Mike to sail with him on his CAL 25. He must have enjoyed the experience because he raced in the CAL 25 Class for twenty years, eventually becoming commodore. When one of the members of the class criticized Mike's lack of decorum one year, he showed up at a class meeting dressed in a jacket with gold epaulets, an admiral's hat and sword, upon which all future CAL 25 commodores in this fleet have had their names engraved.

Mike had a degree in Biology and thought about becoming a physician's assistant. He decided instead to become a paramedic and did so in 1992. This much-needed expertise, combined with his well-developed sailing skills, launched his career as a professional sailor. In 2006, for example, he was at sea about 140 days. His first pro job was with Bill Alcott on the Nelson Merak 68 turbo, EQUATION. Mike was hired on the spot in Tortola, BVI. Another of his early professional jobs was aboard the Roy Disney boat, PYEWACKET. Mike believes that it is essential, if you want to become a professional sailor, to get experience racing in a one-design, dinghy class such as the Melges 24.

He's usually hired as a tactician or strategist. On the big boats, he's the mainsail trimmer.

He has been very active in Match Racing for five years and has won the 2007 U.S. Match Racing Championship. For the last three years, he and his team, Chris & John VanTol, are ranked first in the U.S. and have the highest ranking of any other member at Bayview Yacht Club in Detroit. Match racing is one of the true tests of a sailor's skill because you must race in a variety of boats in approximately ten races per day for a total of thirty races in a weekend

PIED PIPER
Dave Jochum-Bowman/Naval Architect

Dave Jochum first learned to sail when he was in the eighth grade and began racing dinghies at his local park district. His first race was at Waukegan Yacht Club sailing aboard EL TOROS. He remembers it being pretty cold and windy and, for a while, he was intimidated. After he settled down, however, he ended up doing pretty well. After that, he was hooked.

He became a Junior Sailing Coach and captain of his high school sailing team. College sailing at the New York Maritime Academy and the University of New Orleans followed. In 2000, Dave competed in the Collegiate National Team Racing Championship at Eckerd College, FL, and the following year in the 2001 Collegiate Sloop Nationals in Bay Waveland, MS.

As a bowman aboard PIED PIPER, won the 1998 BVI Regatta in Tortola, the 1999 Chicago to Mackinac race with a first-in-class and first overall and winning the Chicago NOOD in 2006. One of his most vivid memories of a Chicago MAC Race occurred in 2005 when the worst lightning storm he has ever experienced struck while he was going through Gray's Reef.

He says that he has been fortunate to only sail aboard PIED PIPER in the GL70 Class because he's been told that its crew is better looking! He feels the qualities needed to win Mackinac races are: an athletic and knowledgeable crew, a capable afterguard (tactician), good sails and proper boat preparation. He likes to compete and finds the foredeck on a GL70 very complex and challenging.

PIED PIPER
Eric Jochum-Halyards

Eric started sailing when he was eight years old at Lake Arlington in Arlington Heights, IL. He never raced until the first semester of high school where he sailed for Loyola Academy in Wilmette, IL for seven semesters. His team qualified for the Baker Nationals in 2006. The Team Racing National event was hosted at Martha's Vineyard, where they took tenth place. It was the first time in four years that the team had qualified.

During the summers, Eric sailed on various boats ranging from J22s, to Melges 24s, to Beneteau 40.7s. In addition he taught sailing for two summers while designing the entire curriculum for the program. He is a member of the Fordham University team which sails on Eastchester Bay near the school located in the Bronx. It is comprised of sailors from across the country, including Southern California, Seattle and Chicago in addition to the NY/NJ area.

During both his Freshman and Sophomore years, they won the MAISA Club Championships, making Fordham arguably the best club team in the MAISA conference.

Beginning at age fifteen, Eric spent five years aboard PIED PIPER. His first race was the Chicago, IL to Hammond, IN mid-distance race. The wind was blowing about 25kts and it was a great thrill for someone who had never sailed on the boat before. He has sailed five Bayview Mackinac races and five Chicago Mackinac races on PIED PIPER in addition to several NOOD regattas and Verve Cups.

PIED PIPER
Perry Lewis-Watch Captain/Helmsman/Sailmaker

Perry grew up in the Chicago area and spent up to seven weeks each summer cruising on Lakes Michigan, Huron & Superior. He learned to hate orange juice as a kid because it made him seasick day after day. Although he was an experienced sailor, he did not begin racing until late in his college career at the University of Chicago, where he obtained a degree in Mathematics in 1975.

His first job upon graduation was as the boat captain of the previous America's Cup 12-meter HERITAGE. This was followed by three years working on a variety of racing boats in the Caribbean and the Pacific. Subsequently, he went to work for North Sails and has remained there ever since. As he puts it, "I've never had a 'real' job."

Over the years as a sailmaker, Perry realized many successes on the racing circuit. They include: North American Champion in S2 7.9 Class (4-5 times), MORC, 1/2-Ton, 3/4-Ton, 1-Ton, J/30, and Tartan 10 (twice). He has been on winning USA teams in the Kenwood Cup (Hawaii) & Sardinia Cup (Italy). No stranger to Mackinac racing, he has been a class winner ten to 15 times.

PIED PIPER
Andy McCormick-Navigator/Helmsman

Andy began sailing dinghies from age eight on Wolf Lake. Right out of college and ever since, he has spent his entire sailing career as a highly valued member of the racing teams of Dick and Jack Jennings. He began as shore crew on the SORC deliveries and was an original crew member aboard PIED PIPER. Like Bob Wiesen, he is a double Old Goat.

He was initially shocked at the downwind speed of the GL70. After twenty five years of racing aboard her, however, he takes the thrill of her speed for granted. He doesn't feel she has ever been over powered. Over the years, he and others have tried to shave off some of the boat's weight by bringing dried food and large jugs of water for the crew to share. Like every other member of the 1987 crew, he remembers the great celebration at the Grand Hotel when breaking the Chicago to Mackinac speed record.

Andy attributes the tremendous success of PIED PIPER over the years to the meticulous preparation prior to each race. The strategy was always to out-prepare the competition.

Nonetheless, he continues to enjoy GL70 racing because of the severe competition among these skippers who have raced against one another for 18 years.

PIED PIPER
J.B. Schumaker-Mid Bowman/Sailmaker

After sailing Optimists, J.B. began to race some double-handed boats such as the club 420 when he was 14 years old. His first year, he placed second for the season locally and won the area E. Bemis trophy. Later he was "Skipper of the Year" and won the season including the Bemis qualifier, which was a very big confidence builder for him. He also sailed Lightnings for some time between his 420 events. His team qualified for the Lightning Junior Worlds in Rochester. He learned a lot at this event about how big this sport is internationally and he also picked up some ideas from others about how to make these boats go fast. He had many great coaches when sailing in the Bayview Yacht Club junior sailing program. One of these coaches, Nathan Hollerbach, became an All-American at the College of Charleston. His other outstanding coach who brought him to another level of sailing was a great sailor, Maria from Denmark.

He does a lot of match racing with Mike Hoey. It is this diversity in sailing which really keeps his interest peaked. His biggest learning curve took place the summer he sailed primarily on the east coast during his last year of junior sailing while competing in Buzzards Bay, Hyannis, in the 420 Nationals, and Bemis Semi Finals. He was 17 years old and was gone all summer doing nothing but big fleet racing. There were 75-100 boats on the line at each event. His most significant victory was winning his first Mackinac Race on a J105, DETOUR. He felt it was most significant because, in long distance racing, you really have to push yourself the entire race while never knowing where your competitor is.

PIED PIPER
Dave Shriner-Helmsman/Trimmer/Rigger

Dave's sailing background in his own words:

"I have been lucky that sailing has always been in my life. My mother and father took me out sailing the first week of my life on our family boat, After that, most of my weekends were spent either day cruising with the family or, once I got older (age seven), my dad graciously brought me along with him for some weeknight racing on Anchor Bay (someone had to fetch the beers).

I really took to it and it has become the passion in my life.

One of the things that has been really great about sailing for me is that I have been taken under many industry professionals' wings and been afforded the opportunity to learn about many different aspects of our sport.

When I was 14, I started riding my bike to work at the then Boston-Doyle sail loft, which was located in a suburb of Detroit and run by Skip Boston. There, I got my first true peek into what goes on inside the sport of sailboat racing. I worked there on and off doing various jobs including cutting out sail numbers, building new sails, learning the art of a GOOD repair as well as helping with the design of new sails. From then on, I was hooked.

Since then I have worked in boat building shops learning about the structure of sailboats and I have headed up some substantial rebuild projects. Presently, I spend my time working at the world famous, Thomas Hardware Company in Grosse Pointe, MI as one of the shop's riggers. I also serve as the coach to Grosse Pointe South high school's sailing team. This, by far, is the most rewarding thing I get to do in sailing. I have coached junior sailing programs and have had coaching positions on big boats, but now I am able to give back to the sport that has given so much to me."

PIED PIPER
Eric Vigrass-Trimmer/Helmsman

Eric narrates his sailing history in his own words:

"I grew up sailing in Port Huron. I started on my father's six meter when I was four years old. My family is a huge part of sailing for me. I have five uncles who own boats all at the P.H.Y.C. The yacht club is a very close-knit group which also allowed me to sail every weekend even if my dad or relatives weren't racing.

I have raced everything from Lasers to Santa Cruz 70s, buoy races to distance races, match racing, and even had some success single-handed racing on my dad's boat. I started on the bow of the boat and only in the last five or six years have found myself moving towards the back of the boat.

The Cal 25 fleet was my first experience in big fleet, one-design racing. After that, I had the opportunity to sail S2 7.9s for a while. I have done a lot of PHRF racing with my dad on his SR33 which is one of my favorite boats to sail. Lately, I have been sailing Mumm 30s, Ultimate 20s, Melges 24s and Santa Cruz 70s on a regular basis.

I can't really pick one moment that's most memorable to me. There have been so many. The most important memory of sailing that I have is spending time with my friends and family, doing something that I love. I think this sport has really taught me a lot about teamwork, competitiveness and life in general. Sometimes I wonder to myself, "What do people who don't race sailboats do with their summers?"

PIED PIPER
Bob Wiesen-Pit Man/Provisioner/Cook

Bob Wiesen began sailing in 1968 at the age of 25. Beginning in 1969, he commenced his sailboat racing career on a Palmer Johnson 43. Bob was an original crew member aboard the PIED PIPER GL70 upon which he raced in each of the two 600 mile races from Port Huron to Chicago, held in 1975 and 2000.

In 2006, he became a Double Old Goat. The significance of this designation is that he has participated in 25 or more Chicago and Port Huron to Mackinac Races. Many Mackinac racers strive to have an Old Goat Designation, which is awarded by the Island Goat Society for 25 years on the Chicago to Mackinac circuit and the Bayview Yacht Club for 25 years on Port Huron to Mackinac Races. Bob's achievement in both races is highly unusual and only shared with a very few other sailors.

PIED PIPER's first ten years on the Great Lakes were record breakers. Bob knows Dick Jennings is a meticulous planner. In addition to a keen eye for boat design, weight distribution, proper equipment and maintenance, sail integrity, and the relationship these components have to overall performance, Dick is also tough on the crew regarding unnecessary weight within personal sea bags taken on board. Dick and Jack have a three-pound-per-person weight limit with carry-on gear on all distance races and a lesser weight allowance on day races. For example, you may bring shoes or boots, but not both.

When asked what has attracted him to distance racing all these years, Bob will tell you that once on the boat, all pressures of the job and thoughts in the mind shift to one focus: "win the race." Everything else is forgotten. "When you are heading out to sea on a meticulously prepared race boat with up-to-date sails and equipment and a top-notch crew to do battle with strong competitors and the elements, you mold with the environment and establish an inseparable relationship with the boat, crew, water, sky and wind. What on earth could be better?" He also enjoys the camaraderie and life long friendships with sailors which have evolved over the years.

BLOW 'EM TO SMITHEREENS
Richard Jennings-Skipper

Richard Jennings has done about everything a person could accomplish in the pursuit of yacht racing. Over a period of 45 years, he's been out there nationally and internationally, racing with and against the best in the sport.

It all began at age 11 when his dad built a sailing dinghy which Dick sailed in Jackson Park Harbor located on the South side of Chicago. He sailed the boat blindfolded from time-to-time so that he could develop a feel for the wind. While hanging around the harbor, he made a connection with the owner of a Rhodes 38 wooden sloop and learned more while working on the boat. At age 15, in 1961, Dick crewed in his first Chicago to Mackinac Race aboard Dick Kaup's boat, BLUE HORIZON. They were the overall winner that year and because of his young age, his dad had to drive him to the awards ceremony. He continued to sail on and perform every task on BLUE HORIZON until 1967 when it finished second in the Chicago Yachting Association's Boat of the Year Award.

In 1968, Dick graduated from Purdue University and began graduate school, only to learn that the vice president of his father's company, Smithereen, (a third generation family-owned pest control company) suddenly died and Dick had to step in. In 1968 and for the next three years, Dick raced his own boat in the Chicago to Mackinac Race. A Soverel 28, named BALDER (son of Oden, God of the sea), it was the smallest boat in the race. Dick and his crew of five faced the storm of 1970, the most violent in the race's history, and were able to find a safe haven in Manistee, Michigan.

In 1970, Dick's parents traveled on vacation to the Netherlands. Dick had heard of Walter Huisman, a Dutchman who was one of the first boat builders to build aluminum racing sailboats. Dick asked his dad to visit Walter while in Holland and check out the quality of his boats. His dad was very impressed. Dick was looking for a boat he could race under the One Ton racing rule. Based upon his dad's recommendation, he traveled to Holland and made the purchase of a terrific racing boat with the very limited financial resources he had at the time. Although originally looking for 33' boat, he eventually bought a 39' boat from Walter which was being offered for sale by its German owner.

Dick really studied the dynamics of sailing and knew what made boats go fast. Despite the high cost of purchasing this boat in Europe and transporting it to Chicago, Dick knew it would compete very well on the Great Lakes. He asked his dad what he should name his new boat. Being in the pest control business, he recommended the perfect name, "PIED PIPER." This boat and all subsequent boats owned by the Jennings family have been named PIED PIPER. The investment paid off with a second place finish and third overall in the 1971 Chicago to Mackinac Race. In 1973, he was the overall winner and PIED PIPER won Chicago Yachting Association's Boat of the Year honors.

During these years, Dick's dad agreed to come out of retirement and work two to three days per week in the family business. This allowed Dick to pursue his racing interests. Dick is now doing the same for his son, Jack.

In 1975, Dick had a boat built in partnership with Lowell North, the founder of North Sails. During this time, John Rumsey, who had known Dick since 1969 and worked for North Sails in San Diego, suggested that Lowell and Dick become partners. This 35-foot boat, designed by Doug Peterson and built by Carl Eichenlaub in San Diego, was designed for the one ton racing class. Lowell could look at a sail and know we should take 3/8" off a seam to make it right. He was a scientist and was totally focused on sailing. He and Dick complimented one another. Their maiden race was 600 miles from Detroit to Chicago via Mackinac Island. This is a race held only once every 25 years. They had the boat trucked to Mount Clemens, MI for the Port Huron to Mackinac, the first leg of the race. Although the boat was shipped to the correct place, the sails were mistakenly shipped to Dallas. When the error was discovered, they were flown to Detroit's Metropolitan Airport, reloaded onto a private plane and delivered to the boat with two hours to spare via the Port Huron airport. They finished third in their class.

The next weekend, Lowell and Dick sailed the Chicago to Mackinac Race which was a light wind race. The boat excelled in light air and won by six hours in class and was the 21st boat to finish overall. This was a remarkable feat for a 35' boat. They shipped the boat to Newport, RI and won the World One Ton Championship in September of 1975, after winning the North American Championship.

Ted Turner had raced against them in Newport and lost. He decided to buy the boat from Dick and Lowell and had it shipped to Australia in order to compete in the Southern Cross Series. He invited Dick to become helmsman for the annual Sydney to Hobart Race. They finished in third place. While Dick was steering in a strong downwind breeze during that race, the spinnaker downhaul broke causing the boat to go sideways to the following waves. Turner became very upset about the incident. Dick apologized and Turner said, "That's OK. I know you're trying hard. With you SOBs up here on deck, I'm going down below to write my will." Dick told him to leave him with the cash, because he hadn't paid the balance owing on the boat. They missed winning the race by ten minutes while ghosting up the river to the finish line. They had a great New Year's Eve party and were joined by Dick's bride-to-be, Gwyn, who flew down for the occasion. They had their honeymoon three months before the wedding.

Turner bought the Atlanta Braves later that year and asked Dick to race the boat on his behalf while he traveled with the baseball team. That Spring in Annapolis, Dick came in third in the National Championship.

In 1977, Dick brought his Dutch boat to the Southern Ocean Racing Conference (SORC) and placed second to Ted Hood. Two years later, he sold the aluminum boat in 1979 after having had two successful campaigns.

In the Summer of 1980, Dick hooked up with Tom Dreyfus from New Orleans and they became partners in a new 43' Doug Peterson design named, LOUISIANA CRUDE. Dreyfus partied hard and, on one occasion, was late for an SORC Race. In order not be left behind, he climbed aboard the boat while it was in the starting area after getting a ride on a reporter's helicopter and jumping into the ocean.

In 1981, Dick and Tom won the SORC by the largest margin in the history of the series. They were disqualified, however, along with the second and third place finishers, skippered by John Kolius and Dennis Connor respectively, for measurement violations.

A month later, a phone call came from the U.S. Yacht Racing Union (USYRU) to ask about the measurement of the boat which was done in New Orleans prior to the race. The measurer in New Orleans said it was correct, but a competitor swam under the boat during the awards ceremony in Nassau harbor and said it had a hollow in the hull that permitted it to act like a catamaran. Because of the competitor's accusation, the USYRU invalidated Louisiana Crude's handicap certificate, thus denying Tom and Dick the 1981 SORC Championship.

In response, Dick brought the USYRU up on Amendment 14 before the American Arbitration Association. The hearing was conducted 1-1/2 years later and Dick lost the case. Subsequently, there was terrible press about Dick and Tom alleging that they were cheaters. Although the second and third place finishers did cheat, Dick was unable to prove his innocence because the boat was sold immediately after his victory to a buyer from Sweden who raced it in the 1981 Admiral's Cup with the same handicap as assigned by USYRU.

CHANCE
Mike Brotz-Owner/Skipper

Mike is the owner of CHANCE, out of Sheboygan, WI. In 1949, Mike Brotz's uncle bought a Herreshoff 87' racing sloop. It was an M Class boat originally intended to become a new America's Cup boat. Built in 1929, it was renamed SABRE and was later converted to a yawl. In 1959 to 1960, Mike and his brother started their sailing careers living and working on the boat during the summer. Docked at Navy Pier in Chicago, she was used for company outings for customers. Mike and his brother also raced on her in the Chicago Mackinac and Queens Cup races.

In 1961 during a freak storm, the boat, which was on a mooring in Sheboygan Harbor, broke off and washed onto the beach. It became dismasted, but the hull was not compromised. It was pulled off the sand and totally retrofitted. Later, the boat was sold and left the Great lakes.

Over the years, Mike has owned other boats including a Lightning which he sailed and crewed with other friends. In 1994, he bought a 44' IOR one-off racing boat which he raced in the years 1994 to 1996 in Mackinac

Races and Queen's Cup Races. He also owned a Tartan
10 for five years which he used as a day sailor.

In 1996, he thought about, perhaps, buying INSATIABLE or
the 50' boat, EQUATION. While sitting at the bar in his yacht
club one evening, Terry Kohler and Peter Reichelsdorfer talked
him into bringing another SC70 to the Great Lakes. They told
him it was easy to sail, had a very straightforward design and
more boats were becoming available for sale on the West Coast.
They stuffed the specs into Mike's pocket about one of the SC70's
which was for sale named, CHANCE. Later that year, Mike
went to San Francisco Bay to watch the SC70's performance
in the Big Boat Series Race. Bill Lee, the SC70 designer and
builder was racing MIRAGE and took Mike to dinner to discuss
CHANCE. Three non-sailing investors had lost the boat to a
bank. It was being used for race chartering. Mike bought her and
the summer of 1997 was his first season aboard CHANCE.

He feels that the people who acquire these boats really appreciate
the ability to own a big boat which is fast and still provides
a chance to get to the island first. The boats are remarkably
straightforward but take some knowledge to handle. They
are, after all, an ultralight with not a lot of ballast. They need
perseverance when the wind is on the nose. When steering, you
must fall off a little. In downwind conditions, however, the faster
the wind is, the faster they go. He likes the way the class was put
together—with rules designed according to a loose box rule.

His son and daughter have raced in all his races with him. In
2007, Mike's wife raced the Chicago Mackinac Race. His family
usually delivers the boat from one racing venue to another. The
family involvement has been his driving force to keep the boat. If
Mike's family would lose interest, he'd sell.

EVOLUTION
Terry Kohler-Owner/Skipper

Terry Kohler, the owner of EVOLUTION, first sailed at the age of five, at his aunt's house in Pentwater, MI on a 16' Herreshoff. At the age of nine, his mother moved to Florida and he spent from 1943 to 1945 sailing with his stepfather through the Florida Keys. Although, he spent five years in prep school so he could be accepted into the U.S. Naval Academy, he decided not to attend. Subsequently, he was accepted at Northwestern University and enrolled in the Navy ROTC program. After only seven months there, he wrote a letter to his superiors saying that he was obviously too immature to continue his college education at this time. Immediately upon leaving school, he arrived in Miami, Florida just in time to participate in the 1954 Southern Ocean Racing Conference's (SORC) annual regatta.

In 1955, he enlisted in the U.S. Air Force and became a B-47 Strategic Air Command (SAC) pilot. After his five-year tour of duty, he enrolled at The Sloane School of MIT where he obtained an undergraduate degree and a master's degree in Industrial Management. During this period, Terry began assuming a leadership role in the family business, The Vollrath Company. In 1963, this allowed Terry's father, at age 66, to pass the business to the next generation. Although Terry entered the business at the age of 29, he did not take the title of president until he was 40.

In 1984, he was presented with a unique opportunity. A friend of his, Peter Barrett, was president of North Sails. Lowell North, another friend who had beaten Terry in the 1978 Canada's Cup

and is the founder of North Sails, asked Peter to find a buyer for
his company. Peter called Terry and asked if he would like to buy
North Sails. Terry, who had recently purchased North Sails for
his boat said, "No, the sails I just ordered last fall are just fine."
Peter responded, "I'm not talking about buying a set of sails. I
am offering to sell you the company." Terry was shocked and
somewhat excited about the idea. North Sails was already the
leading sailmaker worldwide and enjoyed a great reputation in the
sport. He brought the proposal to the Vollrath board of directors
and, much to his surprise, it later approved the acquisition. Since
then, the company has enjoyed tremendous success and has been a
leading innovator in the manufacture of sails.

Terry just loves "being out there" and is a very competitive
yachtsman. He refers to the GL70 owners as Corinthian
Competitors. They love to compete and winning is a bonus. The
Royal Corinthian Yacht Club defines Corinthianism as:

"Corinthianism in yachting is that attribute which represents
participation in sport as distinct from gain and which also involves
the acquirement of nautical experience through the love of the
sport rather than through necessity or the hope of gain."

In 1990, Terry decided to charter a Santa Cruz 70 for the Big
Boat Series of races in San Francisco Bay. Dick Jennings bought
one four years prior in 1986, followed by Bill Martin, who brought
the second SLED (as the GL70 is often called) to the Great Lakes
in 1988. After a successful trial in San Francisco, Terry bought
the third SC70 to come to the Great lakes and re-named her,
CYNOSURE. He raced against the other two for the first time in
the 1991 Chicago to Mackinac Race.

After owning CYNOSURE for nine years, he sold her to John
Nedeau, who renamed her WINDANCER, and he purchased his
second GL70, EVOLUTION in 2000. Upon completion of the
2007 season, Terry has completed 35 Chicago to Mackinac and 18
Port Huron to Mackinac Races. Although he has a busy schedule,

he always makes time for these two races with longtime friends aboard EVOLUTION.

EVOLUTION
Peter Reichelsdorfer-Co-Skipper

Pete got into sailing when he joined the Sea Scouts at the age of 14 in 1949. He lived just three blocks from the yacht club in Sheboygan, WI. At the age of 16, he met a fellow Sea Scout who was the boat boy for an 87' sailing yacht named SABRE. His job was to work on maintaining the boat during the season. He asked Pete if he would help him with his duties on the boat. Eventually, Pete became a paid employee and worked on SABRE throughout his college years. This money helped him pay for his college tuition. While attending the University of Wisconsin, he became a member of the school's sailing team. Upon graduation, he joined the U.S. Navy and became an Officer of the Day aboard a destroyer.

After his tour of duty, he returned to Madison for a master's degree in Mechanical Engineering. The Harken brothers, who went on to build a very successful marine hardware business, were classmates of his. He lived in the Baltimore area for a while and sailed a 26' auxiliary sloop, which he owned, on Chesapeake Bay. On a trip back to the Midwest, he met Terry Kohler at the Chicago Yacht Club. Subsequently, he and Terry raced together on the 1950 Chicago Mackinac Race aboard SABRE. That race was his first long distance race during which he washed dishes, was on watch and hauled canvas sails. Pete says, "Once it gets in your blood, you gain confidence and want to come back."

Pete has held the titles of Commodore of the Sheboygan Yacht Club and Commodore of the Lake Michigan Yacht Racing Federation, which is a governing body for disputes (protests) between competing sailors.

His longest Mackinac Race was 83 hours in elapsed time. His most memorable Mackinac experience was when

EVOLUTION was in front of the pack under the Mackinac Bridge. HOLUA was on her port hip and COLT 45 was on the starboard bow. A very powerful squall came through from the west, bringing other boats up with it. EVOLUTION had taken her chute down in anticipation of the storm. When it hit, COLT 45 broached and HOLUA finished just ahead of EVOLUTION. Seven of the other GL70s finished within three minutes of one another in 50 mile winds. He has raced in 42 Chicago to Mackinac Races and 24 Bayview Mackinac Races.

EVOLUTION
Dan Reichelsdorfer-Co Skipper

Here is a profile on Dan Reichelsdorfer, one of the principals aboard EVOLUTION, in his own words:

"The year was 1973 when my parents purchased a used Cal 2-30 and our family love of sailing began. At first, we as a family cruised the Great Lakes while my parents raced with our local race fleet in Sheboygan, WI. After three years, a bigger boat was needed and ARKTOS, a C&C Redwing 35 was purchased. This boat remains in the family.

I began to sail a Penguin that my father restored in our garage with my brother and me in 1975. Then I moved on to the Sea Scout program and sailed FJs and 470s. The great thing about this program was its emphasis on seamanship. My first competitive sailing was in1976 as part of the crew of ARKTOS in the Sheboygan Yacht Club racing offshore fleet. I was 11 years old and I was hooked.

After that, I also started to race outside the SYC, including the Chicago Mac. My first Mac was in 1984 on AGAPE TOO,

Terry Kohler's fourth boat, but my first charge. Terry chartered INVICTUS, a G&S 45 in 1985, and I cared for her and did my first Bayview-Mac that year. From 1986 through 1990, Terry joined us aboard ARKTOS for the Macs, Queen's Cups, 100 Milers and other offshore races in the Great Lakes.

In 1991, CYNOSURE, a GL70, was purchased by Terry and I became her captain. This was my first big project. I went out to Newport Beach, CA. to take her apart and put her on a truck home. We raced CYNOSURE until 2000, when EVOLUTION was purchased. We ran both boats for sail testing every fall until CYNOSURE's sale in 2005 to John Nedeau. EVOLUTION has been raced since 2001, completing the annual GL70 Championship schedule. Between CYNOSURE and EVOLUTION, we have won five GL70 season championships, sailing with pretty much the same crew from the beginning.

Big boat sailing has brought me many opportunities and experiences, but little boats continue to be important to me. In 1988, I bought my first Lightning, SILENT MOVIE. I still own her today, along with a new Allen Lightning named LAKE EFFECT (Allen Boat Works is on the shores of Lake Erie in Buffalo, and when I went to pick her up, it was a horrific snowstorm compliments of the lake). I have competed in the Midwest District since 1988, in ten North American Championships and sailed in several Southern Circuits."

MIRAGE
Rick Woodworth-Co Owner/Co Skipper
Rick began offshore sailing on a boat named DECISION in 1965. She was an Erickson 35 and this was also, at the age of 14, his first Chicago to Mackinac Race. He will always remember the 72 MPH squall which hit in the Manitou Passage while he was one of the foredeck crew. All the sails were down and the crew was lying

on them to reduce windage. He loved it! As Rick says in his own words, "I was probably too young and dumb to realize the danger."

The year 2007, marked his 40th Chicago to Mackinac Race. He has also completed about 20 Bayview Mackinac Races including a victory in a G & S half-tonner in 1979. In that race, he had a great spinnaker run to Cove Island and then a foggy leg all the way to the finish. While listening on his VHF radio, he heard only the names of the larger boats finishing ahead of him. When on the final approach to the island, with the fog burning off and the sun rising, he realized that he was primarily in the company of much larger boats. What a great feeling!

Rick comes from a sailing family. His grandfather sailed in the 30's and 40's followed by his dad in the 50's and 60's. He has continued the family tradition. Both he and his brother have been sailing together for over 20 years and, when their sons were old enough, they brought them along. Rick's two sons began racing at the ages of 12 and 13, and have completed nine and ten Chicago Mackinac Races, respectively. He believes that racing with his boys has been a great experience for both parties. He also feels there is another dividend for the boys. Onboard a racing boat in long distance races, they have come to know other crew members with different life experiences. They have also had to learn to pull together as a team and rely on one another during the tough sailing situations. He has found that owning a GL70 requires time and attention because of its size and age, but it is a great sailing boat and he has really enjoyed being out there with family and close friends year after year.

MIRAGE
Bill Dooley-Co Owner/Co Skipper

Bill Dooley and Rick Woodworth have owned sailboats as partners for years. Bill was never interested in owning one himself, but liked the idea of having a partner. After beginning his sailing career racing lifeguard canoes rigged with sails, as a ten-year-old, he was hooked on sailing.

Bill, a navy veteran, has been an owner in a large number of boats including a Lightning, Columbia 26, Islander 32, T10, Farr 40, Peterson 48, International 50 and a Nelson Merak 43. In 2001, because Rick's kids were getting older, they decided to buy a Santa Cruz 70. They named her MIRAGE. In all, he has done 39 Mackinac Races. In 1985, he won the Mackinac aboard his T10, winning in a large fleet of 20 to 30 boats.

MIRAGE
Eric Joost-Co Owner/Co Skipper

Eric, the third owner of MIRAGE, was a 1987 graduate of Northwestern University.

A college friend's father bought a new sailboat and Eric was asked to help him with the boat in exchange for some food and beer money. It seemed like a fair bargain and he had great fun sailing to eastern seaboard venues including New York, Nantucket, Greenwich Connecticut, Oyster Bay, The Thimbles and Newport.

He didn't begin racing until 1992. Through networking, he met Rick Woodworth and Bill Dooley at a time when they owned a Peterson 48 named SORCERER. Eric lived in Chicago after graduation and began racing with them in his first Chicago to Mackinac race.

One half of the core group they had in 1993 is still together. He feels relationships are central. He wouldn't spend time with people he didn't enjoy. He likes the mix of people he wouldn't have met in any other venue.

NITEMARE
Tom Neill-Owner/Skipper

The year 2007 marked the 34th Chicago to Mackinac Race for Tom Neill, owner of the GL70, NITEMARE. He started sailing on a Sunfish and, as most sailors, worked his way up to bigger boats. He also completed his 16th Bayview Mackinac Race in 2007. As Tom puts it, "Sailing is my passion." He sails as often as he can. Before he became sick recently, he bought a Melges 32 so that he could do more racing in addition to his GL70 events.

In 2007, he and his NITEMARE crew raced since May 20th in PHRF events off Chicago's lakefront and continued until the last race held on September 20th.

He is another one of those sailors who also subscribes to the theory that you shouldn't race to Mackinac Island on a boat shorter than your age. He feels he has been very blessed to participate in the sport of yacht racing as long as he has. He sails with his friends all over the country and says, "It's all about the people."

He bought a Farr 40 in 1999 and raced it in the 1999 Chicago to Mackinac Race.

As he was sitting on the rail while off watch during that race, he told the guys, "We're not going to the island on this boat again." The average age of his crew is 46 years. Since he bought the GL70, he feels it is an entirely different animal. "You can just put the bow down and let the waterline do the work." He feels that the boat is an awful lot of fun in the right conditions, but buoy races are very difficult in a boat this size because you need 26 hands at the corners to turn the boat

Regarding the Association, he says, "We do a good job with our GL70 Association rules. They work very well. There is no arms race between the owners." He also feels Dick Jennings did a great thing with the purchase of COLT 45, thus preserving another boat in the Great Lakes. Tom thanked him for doing so.

He believes Bill Lee, the designer and builder of the Santa Cruz 70 was far ahead of his time. He verified this fact in his own mind on a recent trip to Spain. Tom and his wife traveled to Valencia, Spain for the 2007 America's Cup Race and actually raced aboard AREVA. Although the AC Cup boats are five feet longer and four feet narrower, with a rig 40' taller and 55,000 pounds more weight than a GL70, he concluded they are no faster downwind.

When I asked Tom if he enjoys going for a sail, he replied, "I don't go cruising. For me, sailing is the next starting line."

POROROCA
Gene McCarthy-Co Owner/Co Skipper

Gene McCarthy has been sailing since 1938 when he was ten years old. He and his parents were invited by a friend to go for a Sunday. On that initial voyage, Gene embarrassed his folks by taking over the boat and telling everyone what to do. He just took to the sport naturally.

He became proficient while racing in the Star Class at the Jackson Park Yacht Club which hosted a Star fleet. In 1955, he won the Great Lakes Championship as crew. In 1959 and again in 1974, as skipper, he won the Great Lakes Star Championship. He won his first Chicago to Mackinac Race in 1953 and has raced in a total of 54 CHI MACS. Over the years, Gene was invited onboard many top boats. In 1960, GREETINGS, a 40' wooden cruising boat, won both MACS. One of the most beautiful boats he raced on was a 53' double ender named GYPSY. Another boat, INFERNO, was a C&C 53, which won every race except when it touched a mark with its spinnaker sheet during a Sheldon Clark Race, the last of the year.

His most frightening moment in a sailboat occurred on an Ericson 46, he owned for two years. While returning from the Caribbean, off Cape Hatteras about 200 miles, he was hit by a 60' rogue wave, which lifted the boat approximately

20' into the air. When it landed back in the water, the force of the impact ruptured all the bulkheads. A marine survey later revealed that the boat was a total loss.

In May of 2005, Gene and his partner, Bob Zeman, bought a Nelson Marek 68 from John Nedeau, which was renamed, POROROCA. The Amazon river flows into a bay on the Atlantic Ocean. When there is a full moon and high tide, the river has five-foot waves, which ride 20 miles up the river creating a pororoca, "A God Almighty Noise." This is the only boat in the GL70 Class which is not an SC70. In his first year of GL70 racing, he came in last in every race. Things changed dramatically when POROROCA won the 2006 Offshore Championship for the GL70 class. Gene is now 79 and also believes you should not sail on a boat that is shorter than your age. Even though POROROCA is 68' long, it seems to work out just fine.

POROROCA
Bob Zeman-Co Owner/Co Skipper

Bob Zeman, a co-owner of POROROCA, began his sailing career at the age of 15 on Lake Geneva in Wisconsin. In 1959, he sailed in his first Chicago to Mackinac race aboard a New York 32. He also remembers when he and his brother were altar boys. He sailed with a priest on one of the boats and served at the mass which was said for the fleet. It did not take long for Mackinac racing success to come his way. In his second Mackinac Race, in 1960, he was the overall winner by 12 hours aboard a 10-meter boat called FREEBOOTER.

The year 2007 was Bob's 41st Chicago to Mackinac race. He has done three Bayview Mackinac races and loves the reception of the people in Port Huron. As he describes it, "The Mackinac

Race is like Christmas for them. They are very warm people." He is grateful for the fact that there has never been a person lost when sailing in the Chicago Mackinac race. He was on a boat once, however, with a crewman who died of a heart attack while racing.

Bob feels that the GL70 community is much like an elite fraternity and is the oldest consecutively running class of boats participating in the Chicago Mackinac Race. The owners are real people. No one was born to be a king. As the commodore of The Old Goats Society, Bob has known most of the owners for years.

STRIPES
Bill Martin-Owner/Skipper

Bill Martin began sailing as a graduate student at the University of Michigan, where he joined the school's sailing club. Later, he joined Bayview Yacht Club where he continued his passion for the sport. He and his wife Sally raced a Cal 25 from 1969-76 and won many races around the buoys in Detroit and long distance races on Lake Huron and Lake Erie. In 1999, Sally won the Cal 25 National Championship. Bill has often served as crew and Sally as skipper.

Over the years, Bill has enjoyed an extensive racing career. He always liked Bill Lee-designed boats, beginning with a Santa Cruz 27, which he sailed in regular races to Mackinac and also single-handed Mackinac races.

In 1979 Bill hired the renowned naval architect, Bruce Farr, to design a one-tonner named, DOWNTOWN, which he raced in the SORC and One-Ton Worlds. In 1981, he represented the U.S. on the three-boat Admiral's Cup team and earned a second-

place finish overall in England on a Nelson Marek boat designed
specifically for that event. Both of Bill's boats, DOWNTOWN and
STARS & STRIPES were built in New Zealand by Cookson.

In 1984, Bill had a Nelson/Marek design, an IOR two-tonner to
campaign for the Canada's Cup, the match racing championship
of North America. His second boat named STARS & STRIPES
defeated two other contenders for the right to represent the U.S. vs.
Canada but he lost to Canada in a close series.

In the mid-80's, Bill joined Dick Jennings with the purchase of
the second SC70 on the Great Lakes. Unlike Dick, who moored
his boat in the Chicago area during the season, Bill kept his 70 at
Bayview Yacht Club in Detroit. Once Dennis Conner started to
use the name STARS & STRIPES for his America's Cup boats,
Bill named his sled STRIPES.

The SC70 is the ideal boat for the family, safe and easy to
sail. Bill's favorite memory was during a Bayview-Mackinac
Race in the early nineties, when he was first to finish, first in
class and first overall. He also recalls a very close Bayview
Mackinac with EVOLUTION one year in which they had
about thirty tacks in the last half hour of a Mackinac Race
at night. One of the best parts about sailing STRIPES is that
with a crew of 12-14 it has become a family affair, with Sally
and their two sons, Seth and Mike, part of the crew, along with
many long-time crew members who are "family" as well.

Bill enjoys both the Chicago and the Port Huron to Mackinac
race courses. The latter course usually provides off wind and
upwind opportunities, but the former race course is more scenic.

Another one of his favorite races is the Trans-Superior
Race from Sault Ste. Marie, Ontario, to Duluth, Minnesota,
a distance of 392 nautical miles. Even though the race is
held during the month of August, it can be a very cold
crossing. He has had ice on the deck and on the sails and a
water temperature of 38 degrees. He remembers his crew

members huddled around the engine, trying to warm up.

Bill has sailed actively since the mid-60s and has also been very involved in the governance of sailing, serving as President of the U.S. Sailing Association from 1989-91. He received that organization's highest honor, the Nathanial G. Herreshoff Trophy, for service to the sport in 2003. Bill also served as President of the U. S. Olympic Committee from December, 2003 until the Athens games in August of 2004 and received the McArthur Award, the USOC's highest award for service to the American Olympic movement.

THIRSTY TIGER
Bert D'Ottavio-Owner/Skipper

Bert D'Ottavio began his sailing career as part of a Boy Scout project. He started sailing on a surfboard and has never been without a sailboat, culminating in his latest, the GL70, THIRSTY TIGER. He has owned many boats with the same name. He had a friend, whose boat was named SALTY GOOSE, so he came up with THIRSTY TIGER. Bert owned a 50-foot boat at one time, but became disgruntled with the racing rules that applied to his boat. He watched Dick Jennings bring the Santa Cruz 70 to the Great Lakes, followed by Bill Martin and Terry Kohler. Although, he had doubts such a design could hold together, he became the fourth owner of an SC70. Contrary to his first thoughts about the boat, he has found these boats do stand up to the punishment of racing on the Great Lakes.

Bert is the only GL70 owner who has made extensive modifications to his boat himself. The other owners have made changes by hiring the work out. Included in his modifications are a large cockpit change and the movement of the engine from its location amidships to 12 feet further aft. He has also installed a new Yanmar engine which saved 600 pounds. As Bert puts it, "I can fix anything on the boat." He has never hired a captain, is a certified diver and holds a 100 ton captain's license.

Although, he acknowledges many of the GL70 skippers are great racers, he has also been a winner on many occasions. Aboard his 43' boat, he was the 1983 overall Chicago to Mackinac winner and was overall winner in 1995 in his first year as a GL70 owner.

Many of his boats won Chicago Yacht Club's "Boat of the Year Award." He has done 33 Chicago and 16 Port Huron to Mackinac Races. He has also served as Commodore for the Chicago Yacht Club in 2004 and 2005.

WINDANCER
John Nedeau-Owner/Skipper

John Nedeau, the owner of WINDANCER, can't remember being without a sailboat. The youngest son of his family in Muskegon, MI, he didn't get a bike at the usual age; his father bought him a sailboat instead.

His father, Harvey I. Nedeau, owned an Alden 39 named ROMAHAJO which they both raced in the Mackinac Races. At that time, the Alden 39 was a very fast boat and one of the early finishers in the Chicago to Mackinac Race. ROMAHAJO was one of the first boats to mount a wind pennant atop the mast, but the boat still had no instruments. When encountering shallow water in foggy conditions, John learned to tell by the wave patterns if danger was imminent. Today, he feels that all of the modern instrumentation has taken the seamanship, as well as much of the fun, out of racing.

At 76 years young, the 2007 Chicago Mac was a celebration of John's 60th Chicago to Mackinac Race. Sixty Macs is a record for Mackinac racers and he has no plans to stop. John is famous to all who have sailed a Mackinac race with him for saying as WINDANCER crosses the starting line, "There is no other place in the world that I would rather be right now. "

One of his most memorable experiences as a young man, was a race to Montego Bay, Jamaica aboard SCARAMOUCH, a Fres/Palmer Johnson 53. The wind built to 45 knots and John became very seasick. At the same time, the crew found a leak in the boat and it started filling with water. John's job was to keep his finger in the hole. After racing for six days in these conditions, they lost to another boat by 20 seconds. Over the years, he has enjoyed many racing successes including a title in a Fres 53 in the late 60's and a Mackinac Trophy victory aboard his 12-meter boat INTREPID, a former America's Cup winner.

One of his favorite Mackinac stories came about aboard the current WINDANCER in the 2005 Chicago Mac. WINDANCER, EVOLUTION and HOLUA had been battling for fleet line honors for the last 200 miles of the race. Between the North Manitou Shoals Light and Grays Reef, the lead changed several times. Just prior to Gray's Reef, the faster rated DENALI entered the fight and passed WINDANCER as the boats entered the Gray's Reef channel. WINDANCER quickly went into close course tactical mode and passed the faster DENALI, leading her out of the channel and into the Mackinac Straights. With fellow GL70 HOLUA leading both of them by three minutes, DENALI and WINDANCER fought it out for second across the line with WINDANCER holding off DENALI and allowing HOLUA to escape for a clean first to finish. WINDANCER was third across the line behind DENALI and HOLUA. John laughs when telling the story, noting that HOLUA owes him one for holding off DENALI.

John's current WINDANCER is his seventh boat named WINDANCER. He built his own C&C50 and C&C52 back in the 1970s. The boat referred to as WINDANCER III actually displayed the name INTREPID on the transom as she was the former two time America's Cup winner. He then purchased a Fres/Palmer Johnson 53, similar to Scaramouch, followed by a large 68 foot racer/cruiser. In 1998 he bought his first sled, a Nelson Marek 68, which he later sold to Gene McCarthy and Bob Zeman, which is now named POROROCA.

John and his wife Joan have six children, three boys and three girls, and nineteen grandchildren. Many of his children and grandchildren join him on Mackinac Races.

WINDANCER
Sam Nedeau-Co-Skipper

"I can honestly say, I have no idea of when I first started sailing. My father and grandfather both being avid racers, allowed me access to boats at a very early age. I do not remember not having a boat. I know I had a boat before I had a bike. I have always had access to racing sailboats, both large and small.

The funny thing about my early days of sailing is that it was not my first love. It was fishing and hunting turtles. That is how I spent the majority of my time on the water front as a youth. I am not the best sailor in the GL70 fleet, but I am willing to bet I have significantly more knowledge in the habits of the North American turtle than the rest of the fleet.

In 1976, my father bought me a windsurfer. It was one of the first one thousand windsurfers built and I spent hours and hours on the water with that board. The equipment was not as developed as it is today and sailing at about 110 pounds without a harness left me awfully sore several times, but sailing that board was fantastic. It really hooked me on sailing speed.

In all honesty, before I was ready to graduate on to the larger keel boats, my father pulled me from the junior sailing program at White Lake Yacht Club, where I was sailing butterflies and C-boats and put me onto the second of his long line of WINDANCER's. I was not ready to contribute while racing at just 12 or 13 years old, but I could clean the decks, wash the hull and drive during deliveries. Pretty soon I found myself calling whichever WINDANCER we happened to own "home." I was always racing beginning with the Trans-Michigan (Now called the Tripp Memorial) until the U-Gotta Regatta in Harbor Springs.

I raced my first Mackinac race at the age of 14. All of my Mackinac Races have been sailed aboard a WINDANCER, with the exception of the 1980 race which I did aboard a Nelson Marek 36 named HOT SHOT. I quickly learned that sailing with my family and with the WINDANCER program was much preferred.

Every summer from age 12 to my early 20s I was aboard a WINDANCER. Once in college, I was able to assume the role of HNIC (Head Nautical in Charge). During those years the family owned the former two time America's Cup winner, Intrepid. In

12 to 14 knots upwind the boat was a dream to sail, but in pretty much any other condition it was rather trying. The boat was built solely for day sailing. We had converted it to racing offshore by putting an engine in her, extending the fore triangle up ten feet and installing an interior. That 12-meter was more work than any boat I have ever been around. The work never ended. We broke everything. Rigs, booms, spinnaker poles, winches, decks, trim tabs, and when we lost the rudder we darn near broke the crews will to sail. INTREPID was a fantastic boat, not designed to sail in over 20 knots of wind. It was our mistake for trying to sail her in heavier conditions. Even today, I cannot think of that boat without smiling.

I have raced so many different kinds of boats, it is hard to believe. Without a doubt, however, the best boats I have ever raced, worked on, or delivered are the sleds. It is not just the speed or the size that makes the experience so rewarding. It is the simplicity of the concept. The ULDB concept of removing weight in exchange for more speed is very foreign to my upbringing on the heavy displacement IOR boats. Racing a sled often reminds me of the hours spent on the windsurfer.

In 2001 (I think) I became the Executive Director of the Great Lakes 70s Sailing Association. In 2005, I was inducted into the Chicago Mac Old Goats Society.

The only offshore race on Lake Michigan that I have not won as a crew or skipper is the Chicago to Mackinac Race. We won the Bayview race a few times, but a win in the Chicago Mac has escaped us. That speaks more to our competition than our abilities. In general, the larger boats attract the best sailors, so top to bottom, the big boat classes tend to have the best sailed boats. The GL70s class is a prime example of talent being found from top to bottom.

CONCLUSION

It was a great adventure sailing in the GL70 Fleet and certainly well worth the effort to assemble all the content needed to write this book as I complete my end of the bargain. Things are never as they seem. Although, I thought the boats were unusually narrow for their length, the beam at 15' was certainly adequate. The boats were much faster than I thought and when heeled, very high above the water's surface. The sailing experience on a boat so large and well designed is a unique and memorable experience. It will be quite an adjustment to return to my 30' boat after racing on the 70s.

The expertise of the crew members is remarkable and, unlike most crews on smaller boats, each person can usually perform every position on the boat. Everyone I met aboard PIED PIPER and WINDANCER knew and acted like they were part of something special. The people involved with all ten boats loved what they were doing and exhibited the *Joie De Vivre* expressed by every sailor who is passionate about this sport. They are the epitome of the work hard, play hard culture. The competition on the water and camaraderie ashore between the crews enriches the whole experience.

I am so happy that I got to know so many of these people and was welcomed wherever I went. I have also enjoyed reliving the summer of 2007 as I labored over this book during the following fall and winter months. It just reminds me again of the pure joy of pursuing and finding a way to realize a dream. Whether you are interested in sailing or not, I hope my story awakens in you the real possibility of pursuing your dreams. Thanks for listening,

Tom Ervin